Praise for

"Dave Howlett isn't a person giving prepared speeches. He incorporated our values into the RHB '3rd gear/good guys' philosophy and presented four 90-minute interactive keynotes in one day. The effect on our staff (physicians, nurses, administrators and staff) was remarkable and has been very long-lasting."

—*Jeanette Despatie, CEO of Cornwall Community Hospital*

"As the core of the ABEX structure emphasizes independence, our advisors need to cultivate an exemplary personal reputation. Dave's 'RHB 3-gear' keynote was the highlight of the conference. His presentation was powerful, uplifting and humorous. In fact, one of our seasoned advisors, who cultivates a reputation for withering criticism, said of Dave's talk 'Usually these things put me to sleep, but that was the most engaging talk I've ever attended.'"

—*Jim Pelot, CFO of ABEX*

"I first heard Dave speak about six or seven years ago. I liked the message: it's simple and timeless, and the way he illustrates the whole concept with the analogies of driving is something that's memorable for most people. So I had him come and talk to our staff in the greater Toronto area and then we had him do a cross-Canada tour and do breakfast sessions for all our clients, who are decision-makers from large and small to medium sized companies across the country.

"The feedback overall was very good. I re-engaged him to do a couple of sessions internally again because I believe his message is timeless and very relevant.

"The message of the first, second and third gear can be used in so many different ways. You can use it to drive your sales and to break down silos etcetera."

—*Dianne Hunnam-Jones, District President, Robert Half*

"My vision is a 'lead where you are' mindset among our people. As part of this evolution, I engaged Dave Howlett to conduct three RHB seminars over one day for our employees. I have heard many speakers in my career, but Dave did something that only a few speakers have achieved: he made me pause. His simple and powerful 3-gear RHB concept was easily taken up at all levels and reflected my vision in an entertaining and powerful manner.

"If you are looking for innovative ways to improve morale and increase movement towards your own goals, I highly recommend a Real Human Being seminar."

—*Kelly Kloss, City Manager of Fort Saskatchewan*

"I have hired a number of speakers for events over the years so I know the challenges of trying to find someone who will 'wow' the audience and also reflects the vision and values of the sponsor.

"I recently employed Dave Howlett to deliver a dinner keynote for our annual conference. Dave's humorous and poignant keynote about how anyone can shift gears and be 'one of the good guys' garnered us rave reviews. He tailored the address to our industry perfectly, and we still have people, a week later, contacting us and telling us how impressed they were with that presentation. The RHB '3-gear' concept is brilliant in its simplicity and remarkable in its longevity.

—*Annemarie Pedersen, Industry Communications Director, Canada Beef Inc.*

"We were seeking an international speaker to attract, inspire and entertain a large audience at our first annual fundraising gala. Dave Howlett's uplifting message of Real Human Being was perfect for our needs. Not only did he incorporate our vision into his talk, he made the audience laugh and think. You could actually see the light bulbs turn on as they made both a personal and professional shift from narrow self-interest towards "do the right thing" behavior. I have no doubt the RHB approach will continue to impact attendees and help us solicit their support as we grow. I would recommend Dave Howlett to any association that wants to reward sponsors or generate new supporters."

—*Paresh Mistry, President of Downs Syndrome Awareness of Peel*

connect

—Like A—

Real Human Being

Elsie!

Dave Howlett

LGAA Conference 2018

connect

—Like A—

Real Human Being

How To Break Down Silos,
Boost Collaboration and
Increase Engagement
In Your Organization

Dave Howlett

Founder of Real Human Being Inc.

BRIGHTFLAME
Books By Experts

First Edition. Published in Canada by Brightflame Books, Toronto, Ontario

For information, call 1-416-209-1503
or visit http://www.realhumanbeing.org/Engage/NewBookings.aspx

ISBN (Paperback): 978-1-988179-06-3
ISBN (Kindle): 978-1-988179-07-0

Dedication

This book is dedicated to my wife, Barbara.

Someone once told me, "when I meet another CEO, I judge them by their watch, their shoes, their car, and their partner."

I am fortunate to have an amazing person as my partner and for that, I am continually grateful.

"I've been in a lot of different industries and companies, and the thing I find quite stunning is the fact that people will pay lip service to culture and say 'Yeah, we need a better culture.' They have this sort of airy-fairy idea that it's parties and billiards tables and gift cards and cake and whatever, and that's what it takes to create a 'good culture'.

"But what your rank and file people really, really want in an organization is to be able to come into work, know what it is they need to achieve and actually be able to do it and feel a sense of success in doing it.

"That to me is the golden heart of what it means to have a great culture. Then you add things like parties and cake around the outside."

Steve Malinowski - CEO The Kraus Group

Contents

Preface

If you're reading this book, you likely have a challenge. Perhaps it is getting people from different divisions to work together. Humans have evolved to be tribal in nature and in many companies, Sales hates Marketing, Marketing hates Finance, Finance hates IT, no one likes HR, and everyone hates head office. Your employees also may be of differing generations, cultures or ethnicities. You may also have silos around union and management or staff in the field and back in head office.

So how will I help you to get folks to transcend tribe and collaborate?

I was determined not to write something for a CEO's book-of-the-month club; the book that sits forgotten on the shelf. And so this book is less about data and more about a solution. The best solutions are short, simple and sticky, and reflect the vision of senior management.

You'll read about real people—real human beings—applying a real solution in the organizations they lead to eliminate the tribalism and divisions that were getting in the way of results. You'll learn about the three modes of behavior—what I call "the three gears"—that people operate in, and how to use that language to create a culture where it's OK to call someone on their behavior without criticizing the person themselves. That's a huge step on the way to creating an inclusive culture without silos and turf wars.

As you read this book, think about your vision for your company and about what you could achieve if every employee did more than what they were paid to do. Not because they expected a reward, but because that was the culture of the company. An employee-owned culture where someone who acted in narrow self-interest felt out of place. A culture like this translates into a powerful brand with reduced attrition and increased productivity.

But if we are going to convince the kids, we need to start with the parent.

That's you.

Introduction

"Silos—and the turf wars they enable—devastate organizations. They waste resources, kill productivity, and jeopardize the achievement of goals."

Patrick Lencioni, 'Silos, Politics and Turf Wars'

Getting your employees to work together to achieve your company's goals is probably one of the greatest challenges you face.

Collaboration leads to improved products or services and more innovation. This, in turn, increases your company's profitability and your employees' engagement and job satisfaction.

Engaged employees believe in their organization's mission; they have a desire to make things better; they're respectful of and helpful to their colleagues; they have a willingness to go that extra mile, and they're keen to keep up-to-date with developments in the field.[1]

Without their engagement and collaboration, however, your objectives are nothing more than idle wishes, lofty dreams that have no hope of being realized.

---

[1] *'The Drivers of Employee Engagement'*, Robinson D, Perryman S, Hayday S., Institute for Employment Studies, Report 408, Institute for Employment Studies, www.employment-studies.co.uk 2004.

But no matter how much you (and your company's survival) need it to happen, your people won't collaborate unless they want to.

For that to happen, you'll have to give them a reason to change their behavior and to leave the confines of their departmental or divisional tribe or silo.

Until now, this has been a challenge too far for many CEOs and organizations. As you'll discover in this book, however, there is a very easy way to inspire your people to collaborate. It's a simple yet elegant solution I call the RHB approach, which has already been used to great effect in public and private companies throughout North America for the past eight years.

RHB doesn't involve cost-cutting initiatives or significant capital investment. What it does involve is giving your employees the tools to behave in the best interests of the company and its customers. Each one— male or female- alike—will want to act like one of 'the good guys': the person who does the right thing because it's the right thing to do.

The organizations that have used the RHB approach have found it helps to break down barriers and increase collaboration and engagement among employees and managers alike.

For any change program to work, three things need to be in place.

First, people need to be engaged in the process. Without that, they're just marking time until this initiative blows over or the next big idea comes down from above.

Second, the change has to be real; it has to happen. Often in companies, people make surface changes, but nothing happens under the surface, and six months later it's back to business as usual.

Which brings us to the third essential: 'stickiness'. If change is to have a lasting impact, people still need to be talking about it six months in, and talking about it with engagement and excitement.

Jeanette Despatie, CEO of Cornwall Community Hospital said this of RHB, "I would recommend Dave Howlett and RHB to any leader who wants a spark to knock down silos and move the needle on employee engagement. Many speakers lecture on engagement; Dave actually gets employees engaged."

And Jim Pelot, CFO of Abex said, "If you are looking for a speaker with a powerful message that translates into sustainable behavior change, I'd recommend you book Dave Howlett."

Finally, Nicolas Heldmann of OpenText said, "Six months after Dave gave a workshop to our finance department, I sent some of our top performers to HR for some managerial training. HR called me and asked 'What are these RHB gears your people keep mentioning?' My people had integrated RHB terminology into their diction. This created long-term retention."

Read on to discover how the RHB approach will help you to overcome the barriers or silos within your company so that your employees want to work together to achieve your vision.

Join RHB Nation

I would love to share more with you about the Real Human Being philosophy, approach and models. I have a very active online community where I share news, tips and short 'Gearshift Moment' videos.

You can join the conversation at

www.realhumanbeing.org/facebook

Chapter 1

The Barrier To Growth In Your Company

"When silos are present, individuals, teams and entire organizations are made to suffer."

Dr. Sharon M. Biggs, 'The Silo Effect'

Silo mentality or tribalism is rife throughout many North American organizations. While fierce, even blind loyalty to one's immediate colleagues and leader might once have seemed admirable and necessary, it's more of a hindrance than a help in this age of globalization when companies must adapt and innovate with lightning speed to survive.

That's because this tribalism, or silo-building, creates barriers and stops the flow of information, which decimates a company's ability to compete.

It's also something that customers and prospective customers pick up on. Brad Brooks, the Chief Marketing Officer (CMO) of Juniper Networks, a publicly traded US software company, says as silos solidify, your company starts to show up as disconnected in front of the customer.[2]

As he puts it, "You lose the connective tissue, and customers pick up on things." Needless to say, a disconnected marketing team and company create acute corporate image problems for brands when going to market.

A recent global study of CMOs by Teradata found that silos are present in many of the areas CMOs oversee, both within marketing departments and between marketing and other core functions. According to Teradata, 74% of marketers say that marketing and IT are not strategic partners in their company.

Silos can create a toxic environment in which divisiveness breeds and in which collaboration cannot survive. Take the following examples.

As one financial year draws to a close, a manager commissions a completely unnecessary project to ensure he doesn't lose any of his budget the following year. Another department urgently needs those funds, but the manager needs to protect his current budget to avoid future cuts.

A customer calls, demanding to know when he will receive his product. The sales rep calls the warehouse and is told the shipping information is in the system, but they are not authorized to release it to the customer. Understandably, the customer cancels the order and takes his business to a competitor. He never returns.

A manufacturing company is behind schedule in its latest production batch. The production manager will be

---

[2] 'Breaking Down Marketing Silos: The Key To Consistently Achieving Customer Satisfaction And Improving Your Bottom Line', Seligson, Hannah, Forbes Insight, Forbes Media

penalized if the products are late to market, but the quality assurance manager won't release the test results until the production memo is rewritten in the style she prefers. It causes a two-day delay.[3]

A company has the opportunity to sell telecommunications equipment in China, but the customer wants on-the-ground support from the vendor's IT Department. She also wants a Mandarin-speaking engineer to help her manage the project. Unfortunately, no one in the IT Department will return the phone calls or emails of the salesperson who is trying to close the deal.

Meanwhile, the Engineering Department is stonewalling the deal because its manager is allocating all the engineers who speak Mandarin to a project that will be credited to his department, even though the China-based project offers far better profits for the company.

The salesperson's manager is powerless to get cooperation from either the IT or Engineering managers.[4]

Silos lead to organizational chaos, wasted resources, and lower profits. The energy that should be invested in improvement and innovation to achieve growth is often spent in petty squabbles and turf wars.

In such an unpleasant environment, work becomes a struggle for leaders and employees alike, making it challenging to get people to work together to achieve goals, satisfy customer needs, build market share and earn profits.

---

[3] 'Overcoming Barriers to Success: What creates them? And how can your organization knock them down?', Rieger, Tom, Business Journal, Gallup, Feb 3, 2011

[4] 'Creating Wealth from Talent in the 21st Century Organization: Mobilizing Minds', Bryan Lowell L., Joyce Claudia I., McGraw-Hill

It creates a poisonous environment that destroys your employees' motivation and engagement. That, in turn, takes an enormous toll on collaboration and therefore productivity.

Engagement Goes Straight to the Bottom Line

Engaged employees care about the work they do, and feel connected to their colleagues and the organization they work for. Those who aren't engaged, on the other hand, are effectively sleepwalking through their days, according to the most recent *State of the Global Workplace* report by international advisory and research firm, Gallup.[5] Such employees put time into their work, but not energy or passion. They are indifferent.

However, they're still better employees than the group which Gallup calls the 'actively disengaged'. Those people act out their job-related misery. They undermine what their engaged co-workers accomplish. They're hostile towards their job, their supervisor or manager, and their company. Not surprisingly, they can end up destroying a work unit or an entire business.

"Actively disengaged employees are more or less out to damage their company," warns Gallup. "They monopolize managers' time; have more on-the-job accidents; account for more quality defects; contribute to 'shrinkage', as theft is called; are sicker; miss more days; and quit at a higher rate than engaged employees do. Whatever the engaged do—such as solving problems, innovating, and creating new customers—the actively disengaged try to undo."

---

[5] 'State of the Global Workplace: Employee Engagement Insights for Business Leaders Worldwide', Gallup, Inc., www.gallup.com, 2013

Right now, you might be thinking, "I'm so lucky *my* employees aren't like this." Think again. Your employees are probably *exactly* like this: as the most recent international Gallup poll shows, only 30% of workers in the United States and 16% of workers in Canada consider themselves to be 'engaged' or emotionally invested in—and focused on—creating value every day for their organizations.

So what about the rest?

Well, according to the same poll, 52% of employees in the US and 70% of employees in Canada say they are 'not engaged' in their jobs. A further 18% of American workers and 14% of Canadian workers say they are 'actively disengaged' with their jobs.

Unfortunately for their employers, just because someone is disgruntled at work, that doesn't mean they will leave the job they hate so much. Many of them stay put and continue to wreak havoc on productivity and relationships, according to an engagement study conducted by Psychometrics Canada Ltd.[6]

You might wonder what difference any of this makes to your bottom line. After all, there will always be whiners and complainers. How important can a few disaffected employees be, really?

Actually, it's hugely important, because a highly engaged workforce means the difference between a company that thrives and one that struggles, according to Gallup and others who measure organizational performance.

---

[6] '*Control, Opportunity & Leadership: A Study of Employee Engagement in the Canadian Workplace*', Psychometrics Canada Ltd., www.psychometrics.com, 2010

Companies with engaged employees flourish. Employee engagement is strongly connected to business outcomes— such as productivity, profitability, and customer satisfaction—that are essential to an organization's financial success.

When employees are engaged, they're passionate, creative, and entrepreneurial, and their enthusiasm fuels growth. They're emotionally connected to the mission and purpose of their work. They drive innovation and help move the organization forward.

Companies with engaged employees outperform companies with a disengaged workforce by 147% in earnings per share and realize:

- ✓ 41% fewer quality defects
- ✓ 48% fewer safety incidents
- ✓ 28% less shrinkage
- ✓ 65% less staff turnover (low-turnover organizations)
- ✓ 25% less staff turnover (high-turnover organizations)
- ✓ 37% less absenteeism.

Highly engaged employees can improve business performance by up to 30%, according to Hay Group Insight's workforce opinion surveys.[7] They're also 2.5 times more likely to exceed performance expectations than disengaged employees, the Hay Group's employee and customer survey division found.

"A well-aligned workforce results in better bottom-line performance," it says. "It delivers higher scores on business-critical key performance indicators such as profit, innovation or safety. It also means comparatively better share-price performance."

---

[7] 'Highly engaged workers create better financial performance', Hay Group Insight, www.haygroup.com

In other words, a workforce that is engaged and collaborates rather than fights will be hugely beneficial to your company. You can expect:

- ✓ Improved employee engagement and morale
- ✓ Enhanced workplace productivity
- ✓ Improved competitiveness
- ✓ Improved talent attraction
- ✓ Improved corporate culture
- ✓ Better employee retention
- ✓ A smooth transfer of knowledge from experienced employees before they retire
- ✓ Improved customer experience[8]
- ✓ More effective execution that saves time (through faster decision making) and money (from resource sharing, knowledge transfer, and lower interaction costs)
- ✓ Greater innovation and bolder strategic moves.

Augie Ray, Executive Director of Community and Collaboration at the United Services Automobile Association® says collaboration is critical to any company's survival.[9] "With the pace of change increasing and the risks of moving too fast or too slow never greater, the ability to have employees collaborate effectively regardless of space, time, language and other impediments is no longer just a competitive advantage—it is vital.

"Collaborating effectively inside and outside the organization is the only way to ensure that the enterprise

---

[8] *'How do I drive effective collaboration to deliver real business impact?'*, Dewar Carolyn, Keller Scott, Lavoie Johanne, Weiss Leigh M., McKinsey & Company, 2009
[9] *'The Collaborative Organization—A Strategic Guide to Solving Your Internal Business Challenges Using Emerging Social and Collaborative Tools'*, Morgan, Jacob, McGraw-Hill Professional, Jly 2012

and the employees are prepared for rapid changes in technology, human behavior, and business culture."

It's a view shared by many executives across the globe. In a recent survey of 1,656 executives from 100 countries, most said that collaboration is crucial to the future of their organizations.[10] At the same time, increased collaboration will be a defining feature of the company of 2020.

Executives say they expect to see a lot more collaborative problem solving inside and outside their organization; many intend to create employee incentives to encourage collaboration across functions and with external stakeholders.

Unfortunately, many executives recognize they're still a long way from that ideal. A McKinsey survey revealed that only 25% of senior executives described their organizations as being effective at sharing knowledge across boundaries, even though nearly 80% acknowledged such coordination was crucial to growth.[11]

Social media is forcing the issue, however. The delineations that allowed organizations to have separate functions (such as Marketing, R&D, Sales, and Customer Service, etc.)— and across the entire value chain of stakeholders—begin to break down when the customer's view of your company becomes the prevailing reality, says Joshua-Michéle Ross, writing in *Forbes*.[12]

---

[10] '*Foresight 20/20: Economic, industry and corporate trends*', Economist Intelligence Unit & Cisco, The Economist, The Economist Intelligence Unit 2006

[11] '*The McKinsey Global Survey of Business Executives, July 2005*', The McKinsey Quarterly, www.mckinseyquarterly.com, Jly 2005

[12] '*Collaboration Rules: Five Reasons Why Collaboration Matters Now More Than Ever*', Ross, Joshua-Michéle Forbes, O'Reilly Media, www.forbes.com, Jun 13, 2011

"With the customer's new-found communications power that is exactly what is taking place today," he says.

"Any weakness across the complex customer relationship is potentially exposed to the world. You may have a brilliant marketing campaign but if the product is a loser—you are lost."

Equally, having a brilliant product won't be enough if your customer service is poor since prospective buyers will be forewarned.

"Therefore, any planning exercise in one silo will necessarily require collaboration with the others to have any chance of success.

"While the drivers that make collaboration vital are technical, the solutions are not. Collaboration is, at its root, a social activity. It is founded on generosity, sharing, and openness. As such collaboration begins in organizational culture."

And that's why it is so important that you find ways to overcome all the silos that exist in your company.

How To Knock Down The Barriers To Collaboration

In the following chapters, I'm going to share a simple yet powerful approach to get employees to stop fighting and to work together. It can be used to break down any kind of barrier or silo in your company, whether it's generational, divisional or departmental, management versus employees, union versus management, or Head Office versus branch offices.

The RHB (Real Human Being) approach is designed to bring about deep-seated change in behavior—the very thing that will generate long-lasting positive change within your company and eliminate those costly dysfunctional barriers.

It helps people to overcome the 'Us Versus Them' thinking that is responsible for silos of any kind in an organization. Instead, they begin to look for similarities rather than differences between themselves and their colleagues.

"At its most basic level, this constant analysis of Us and Them governs the way we treat the people with whom we come in contact," writes Jeff Havens in *Us vs. Them: Redefining the Multi-Generational Workplace to Inspire Your Employees to Love Your Company, Drive Innovation, and Embrace Change*.[13] "The more we can identify Us qualities in others, the better we tend to get along; the more we identify Them qualities in others, the more we respond with hesitation, confusion, suspicion, contempt, derision, or outright hatred."

RHB encourages people to look past stereotypes and labels, and treat others as real human beings. It helps them to move from acting in their own self-interest (or in the interest of their department, division or unit) to behaving in the best interests of the organization, other employees, and customers.

"Our preoccupation with differences only heightens our fear and anxiety in a world that's already scary enough," wrote Gretchen Gavett in the *Harvard Business Review*.[14] "The challenge is to look past the stereotypes and listen to one another so that good work gets done efficiently and humanely."

---

[13] 'Us vs. Them Redefining the Multi-Generational Workplace to Inspire Your Employees to Love Your Company, Drive Innovation, and Embrace Change', Havens, Jeff, Pearson Education, 2015
[14] *'Generations United'*, Gavett, Gretchen, Harvard Business Review, www.hbr.org, Jan-Feb 2016

RHB brings about a profound and almost immediate transformation in people's behavior. Time and again, I've had phone calls and emails not just from CEOs and HR professionals, but even employees, telling me how RHB created a deep and lasting transformation in their behavior. I don't know about you, but I can't think of one other method that brings about a dramatic change in people's behavior in such a short time.

You'll find that this method dovetails with others your organization might be using (such as Six Sigma, diversity training, coaching, mentoring, cross-functional teams or something more radical such as a Results-Only Work Environment). What's more, your employees will embrace and adopt it *willingly*.

How can I be so sure?

Because it encourages people to behave altruistically and, as behavioral economics has shown, most human beings are motivated to do the right thing. Individuals routinely forgo narrowly conceived self-interest for the sake of altruistic motives, according to Hetan Shah and Emma Dawney of the UK think-tank, the New Economics Foundation (NEF).[15] Further, people's self-expectations influence how they behave: they want their actions to be in line with their values and their commitments, they say.

In other words, people want to feel as if they're behaving like one of the 'good guys' at work and in life.

It also makes them happier than those who pursue extrinsic goals such as money, image, and fame, according to Richard

---

[15] 'Behavioral Economics', Shah, Hetan, Dawney, Emma, New Economics Foundation, www.neweconomics.org, September 21, 2005

Ryan, a professor of psychology, psychiatry and education at New York's University of Rochester.[16]

Professor Ryan studies human motivation and its effects on psychological wellbeing and is the co-developer (with Edward Deci) of Self-Determination Theory, an internationally researched theory of human motivation, personality development, and wellbeing. His work has shown that people who have decoupled their own sense of self-worth from material possessions or recognition are happier than those who chase money, fame or recognition.

"Our studies all show that an emphasis on materialism does have a cost," Professor Ryan says. "The more emphasis people put on worldly gains, the less happy they appear to be. It's the people who invest in intrinsic, personal satisfactions who are the contented ones."

I've seen the results RHB has helped to bring about. It has been used successfully in major public and private organizations throughout North America. The feedback I've received from CEOs, managers and employees has been overwhelmingly positive.

Joe Vincec said: "We brought Dave in as a guest speaker at our monthly law firm trainers association meeting. He was fantastic. His RHB message is incredible in its simplicity, and that's precisely what makes it very powerful and effective.

"The RHB gears, and specifically the 3rd Gear actions, stick in your mind long after Dave has left the building. The concepts he teaches are universal and can be applied both to personal and work life.

---

[16] '*Money? Thanks but no thanks*', Hauser, Scott, Rochester Review, www.rochester.edu

"For work life, the RHB program is a truly superior 'employee engagement' program. Thank you, Dave, for sharing your RHB message with our group!"

And Christine Walterhouse told me, "Dave, I have had the privilege of hearing more than one of your talks and not only do I find them motivational but—more importantly—down to earth. You provide the audience with practical concepts that relate to our everyday lives. You are a truly what you promote—a real human being."

Moreover, the method is sticky: people are still using it many years after they first encountered it. For instance, four years after hearing my keynote address, Allison Gatey contacted me to say, "I saw your presentation about four years ago when I worked in the private sector. I honestly think of it every single day. That's how your presentation is different, plain and simple. It opens people's minds up and gets people to participate in positive change in a way that is so simple that it becomes almost involuntary. I work in the public sector now, and I often think how much we would benefit from your presentation."

The beauty of the RHB approach is that it gives employees a common language to describe behavior: first gear for narrow self-interest; second gear for reciprocity; and third gear for altruistic or 'good guy' behavior.

I've found that people naturally want to operate in third gear, so they learn to check and then alter their own behavior. They can also use the common language of RHB to call others on their behavior in a way that isn't threatening or in any way demeaning.

President and CEO of the Kraus Group Steve Malinowski has seen this in action in his company. "The genius of Dave's approach, I would say, is that he gives people the language and almost the authority to call a behavior without threatening the identity of the person they're speaking to."

Before joining the Kraus Group, Steve was CEO of Janes Family Foods Ltd, where he also used RHB. Here's how he describes the impact it had on that company.

"Dave helps a company transform its culture into one that spends its energy creating value as opposed to wasting its energy destroying value internally.

"From the time that Dave started working with us to the time that I left Janes, we doubled our sales and almost doubled our profit."

The change in culture was the enabler for a lot of that.

"The cultural transformation we underwent at Janes, and our ability to use third gear for teaching language and breaking down silos, enormously reduced the amount of friction that was there.

"Good CEOs will spend time understanding their products, their market, their customers, their employees, their capabilities and their resources, and they'll get people involved in putting together a great strategy that fits market opportunity. Then it's down to the CEO to ensure the company executes the strategy. But it's just mystifying, and beyond frustrating at times, when you've got an excellent strategy which people have helped create that cannot be executed because people will simply not work together.

"Getting people working together is incredibly important. Inevitably what CEOs hate is when you get half a dozen division presidents or VPs in the room, and it becomes a competition for status and ego as opposed to a competition for 'let's actually create the best thing here, regardless of who looks like the winner or loser'.

"I've been in a lot of different industries and companies, and the thing I find quite stunning is the fact that people will pay lip service to culture and say 'Yeah, we need a better culture.' They have this sort of airy-fairy idea that its parties and billiards tables and gift cards and cake and whatever, and that's what it takes to create a 'good culture'.

"But what your rank and file people really, really want in an organization is to be able to come into work, know what it is they need to achieve, and actually be able to do it and feel a sense of success in doing it.

"That to me is the golden heart of what it means to have a great culture. Then you add things like parties and cake around the outside.

"Dave's methodology and philosophy on third gear and breaking down silos is not a way to create a strategy *per se*, but it is a way of getting people *to work together to create a strategy*. Then, when people execute the strategy and things go wrong—as they inevitably do—Dave's philosophy and third gear are the mechanisms that keep the ensuing friction and blame to a minimum.

"Every Chief Executive thinks to himself or herself, 'There are two things that I need this organization to do: one, we need to ensure that we have a strategy that beats the competition in our current environment and two, we need to make sure that we actually execute on that strategy.'

"Inevitably any CEO who thinks he or she alone can come up with the strategy doesn't deserve to be a CEO. Any CEO who thinks that he or she alone is the one to execute a strategy is worse than delusional. Most CEOs are disconnected from the points where their employees physically produce goods and deliver services. What those employees do at those points are the real moments of truth in an organization, and where the actual economic value is added.

"All any CEO can do is set up the winning conditions for those things to happen. That's the job of the CEO. And so why wouldn't you try to organize the conditions in such a way that makes it easier for you to win?

"Again, the RHB philosophy actually reduces the friction so you can create the strategy that you need and also helps to be able to minimize the friction in executing that strategy so you can create the value.

"Most CEOs have no idea of where they can even start with a cultural transformation. They will go into an organization, and they will recognize that the culture is dysfunctional and that they need to do something.

"They assume donuts on Friday and putting a billiards table in the break room will make people feel better about being here. The reality is that what people really, really need is not a bunch of slogans or value statements plastered in every meeting room that say 'We are going to be the kind of people who act with integrity, who are determined to get the job done and who put our customers and shareholders first.'

"Dave's stuff is not something you put on a poster and place in every meeting room. It's the kind of stuff that says 'No, you really need to take a look at your own individual behavior. Forget what the other guy's doing. It has nothing to do with him. We're not asking you to go out and change all of your colleagues. We're asking you to do one simple thing: look at *you*. What can *you* change? You can change *you*. What gear are *you* behaving in?'

"When you understand what gear you're behaving in, and you can recognize the gears in other people, and you have the collective permission and the non-threatening language through Dave's training to actually talk to one another about behaviors that you don't like, you don't need it up on the wall because people can actually talk to one another and deal with it.

"This is why, in my opinion, Dave's stuff is so powerful. You can reinforce Dave's methodology and philosophy. You can incorporate it—like we did at Janes—into things like performance evaluations.

"If companies are serious about this, then Dave's talk provides people with the seed. Dave's methodology provides people with a language with which to talk about it.

"Companies that are successful in cultural change are then going to need in some way to institutionalize that momentum in their human systems: things like recognition, rewards, hiring, firing, performance evaluations, and so on."

The positive effects of RHB last because it establishes a self-reinforcing behavioral loop in the individuals who adopt it.

Kim Stewart Wilkinson said, "I don't pretend always to think or say the right thing. But what RHB did for me is remind me to take that extra second to think about what my actions may cause. Will it hurt someone, hurt me or be helpful? I still may not always get it right, but I think it has saved me at times and made me a better 'good guy'."

Companies have used the RHB approach to knock down silos of all kinds, boost employee engagement, improve customer service, innovate, and resolve what appeared to be intractable union disputes. Individuals have used the RHB method to collaborate with colleagues in their own and other divisions, improve sales, get better at networking, become more innovative, and enhance their personal relationships.

Chapter 2

First Gear Behavior

"We have always known that heedless self-interest was bad morals; we now know that it is bad economics."

Franklin D. Roosevelt

Growing up, I was a 'military brat', the child of a father in the Air Force. Our family moved from one military base to another every few years. In 1973, my dad was transferred to a Canadian army base in Lahr, West Germany as part of Canada's NATO commitment.

A week after we arrived in Lahr, my parents were keen for us to explore our new home so took my brothers and me for a drive through the local countryside. It was a glorious sunny day, perfect for an outing.

Eventually, Dad parked the car, and we made our way down a country lane. Next to the lane was a German cemetery. It was beautifully maintained with a manicured lawn and flowers adorning the graves.

My mother commented how much she admired the way Germans tended their graveyards.

We wandered on a little further and came to a hillside cemetery. It looked remarkably different from the first. In this one, the gravestones were in disrepair, many overgrown with grass and weeds. There were no flowers and it was obvious that it hadn't been mown in a very long time,

I remember Mom expressing her surprise at the difference between the two cemeteries. It bothered her so much that she said she had to find out why one had received so much attention and the second had been abandoned.

Looking around, she spotted a boy in a nearby field and called to him. In rusty German, Mom asked him why the second graveyard was so poorly tended.

He answered briefly

Mom translated, "He says it's a Jewish graveyard."

My 13-year-old self wondered how people could live and work together, and then turn on one another. How a leader could exploit the fault lines of race and religion to such an extent that 30 years later, certain graves were still untended because no one saw it as their responsibility.

I believe that Real Human Being started that day; that if we treat every person we meet as a human being, rather than prejudging them as a member of a tribe, we all benefit.

But just because your employees are human, that doesn't mean they always do the right thing.

I've discovered that we all tend to behave in one of three ways, or *gears* as I call them.

First gear is narrow self-interest behavior. Companies see first gear manifested among their employees as entitlement, 'not-my-job'-ism and 'us against them' behavioral silos. Societies see first gear exhibited as racism, bullying, homophobia, and ageism.

One aspect of first gear is the need to seek out an enemy: the 'others'.

When Adolph Hitler wanted to create solidarity in his country, he did it by identifying a group of 'others'. They were Jews, gypsies, homosexuals, and the disabled. Then he did everything he possibly could to 'purify' his country of those people.

Second gear is extrinsic reward. Many Germans were anti-Semitic because of second gear incentive systems (peer pressure, desire for promotion and status, or fear of punishment). In a work environment, second gear behavior is when people only do something positive because they'll be rewarded for their actions.

Third gear is intrinsic reward. It means 'doing the right thing'. It means trying to understand the actions of the so-called 'enemy'. It's the realm of 'good guy behavior'—looking past someone's age, generation, tribe, nationality, or gender and connecting with that individual as a human being.

German industrialist Oskar Schindler was operating in second gear when he employed 1,200 Jewish people in his ammunition and enamelware factories during the Holocaust. Later, he demonstrated third gear behavior by doing whatever he could to keep his Jewish employees alive.

And here's the interesting thing about the neglected Jewish cemetery: When we returned a week later, the grass in the graveyard had been neatly clipped. Sometimes, just asking questions can bring about transformations in people's behavior.

Understanding First Gear

Let's look more closely at first gear, the gear of narrow self-interest. It's behavior driven by a mindset of "Me first, me second and anything left over, me again".

I usually ask an audience if they know anyone who behaves in first gear. Typically, they'll look around the room looking for likely contenders and maybe even stare at one person accusingly. It's obvious that they just want to stand up and point an accusing finger at that particular person and yell out, "He does!"

That's when I say, "Hang on a minute, all of us behave in first gear at some stage."

Don't believe me? Just think back to the last time you were on a gridlocked highway and someone tried to squeeze in front of you. If you were in first gear mode, you weren't going to let them in, *no matter what.* Maybe you just inched your car forward just to be sure the other driver understood your intention. All the time, you just stared straight ahead. You made no eye contact whatsoever with the other driver, but the message was clear: *"Forget about it, you ain't gettin' in! Should have gotten up earlier like I did, buddy!"*

First gear behavior manifests in all kinds of ways in the workplace, like taking the last remaining cup of filter coffee in the lunchroom and walking away without replenishing the water or coffee, so the next person in there gets nothing.

"I would fill it up, but I'm in a hurry."

"What water? Doesn't someone get paid to do that?"

"I'm too important to waste time on stuff like that!"

"No-one else was in there."

It's about putting your interests above everyone else's in the company. Like refusing point blank to give a colleague some help.

"Why should I? It's not my job. Anyway, I don't get paid to teach!"

"What's in it for me? Nada, zip, zilch! I don't think so!"

"I had it tough, kid. Why should you have it any easier?"

"You think you're so smart? Then you figure it out!"

"I want everyone to see that you're not up to the job, Pops."

It manifests in more serious ways, too, with divisions and departments acting in their best interests regardless of the impact it will have on the company.

"I don't care what Marketing thinks. We're doing this our way."

"We need to keep the same budget or our department will lose face."

"I'm sorry you've got to get those letters out, but we're packing up for the day. Maybe if you'd asked us a few weeks ago, we could have planned for it."

First gear behavior appears in all industries and all professions. I spoke with a lawyer recently, and he said it's easy to look at a contract and see what kind of mindset it was written in: narrow self-interest, reciprocity or with a 'good guy' mind-set.

A first gear contract, he said, is written in a 'squeeze them 'til they squeal' way. It'll be a very onerous contract with hefty penalties, which benefits only one party. Usually, people start negotiations off in first gear with an "I win-you lose" mentality, before realizing that if they want to reach an agreement, they'll have to compromise.

You'll see first gear behavior in salespeople too. First gear in sales is the reason we get bad images and jokes about salespeople. You only have to type 'salesperson' into Google, and you'll be presented with a thousand pictures of people with insincere smiles.

A salesperson in first gear will run through a list of the product's features and benefits regardless of what the prospective customer wants or needs. Meanwhile, the customer is standing there thinking, *"He hasn't even asked me what I want."*

First gear in sales manifests like this: "I've got to sell this because I want the commission. Who cares what's right for the client? I don't. Why doesn't he just buy the darned thing already so I can get the check?" In other words, *"My best interests are more important than the client's."*

What does first gear behavior look like in Finance? Probably something like this: you call Finance to find out why you haven't been reimbursed for your expenses.

"Oh yes, I remember seeing your claim," says the person on the other end of the phone.

"So what happened? That was a month ago. No, it's longer than that. Where is it?"

"It was three weeks and four days ago actually."

"What?"

"It wasn't a month ago. It was three weeks and four days ago."

"Okay. But it's not showing up in my bank account. Where is it?" Exhale. "*Please.*"

"Oh, it won't show up in your account."

"Why not?"

"Because we didn't process it. It's still here on my desk."

Deep breath. "Okay. Any reason?"

"Because it's not filled out in the right way."

So first gear behavior in Finance can be, "You do it our way or we're not processing it. Deal with it."

Of course, that kind of thing doesn't just happen in Finance. The CEO of a huge food processing plant told me how first gear behavior manifested in his organization.

"There were a lot of production staff and a lot of quality assurance personnel working on the factory floor. Additionally, there were also a number of government officials who were on the floor for every minute that the plant ran," he recalls.

"The government officials include veterinarian inspectors, hygiene inspectors, and food inspectors. They were all part of the operation. They had things to do to ensure the process created an excellent, safe food chain.

"Unfortunately at some point, the head of Production and the head of Quality Assurance (QA) decided they hated each other. It got to the point where they were deliberately doing things to get power over the other.

The head of Production would try very hard to get the QA team excluded from meetings and decisions to make the head of QA look stupid and to lessen his authority.

"The QA guy, in turn, resented that behavior. He said he'd crack down further and force Production to do some things they didn't need to do. He told Production, 'We can force you to do this stuff. Just watch us.'

"It got to the point that the head of QA ingratiated himself with the chief of the government inspection group for the sole purpose of using the government inspectors to force Production to do a whole bunch of things they didn't need to do."

That's a classic example of first gear behavior: two department heads putting their own interests above everybody else's—no matter what the consequences.

Why do people behave in first gear?

Stress is one reason. Quite often, if you're time-challenged, you will drop back to first gear because you're just trying to keep your head above water.

There are a lot of stressed employees who are basically trying to keep their head above water. The 2008 recession created a lot of trauma in the business sector, with redundancies in many industries. That's still having an impact today. Employees are sometimes doing the job of two, even three people but not getting paid any more than they were before the recession. It's understandable when they behave in first gear.

A lack of confidence can be another reason for sliding back into first gear behavior, and so can outright fear.

The behavior of those around you, particularly your supervisors and managers, has a very strong influence on your behavior too.

A CFO came up to me after a talk and said, "I'm trying to be a good guy, but my boss is in first gear. How do I work with him?"

"What makes you think he's in first gear?" I asked. "Give me an example of his behavior." "He takes credit for other people's work."

"Okay, how do you know that?"

"Because I've come to him with a few ideas and then he's passed them off with his name attached to them."

"How does that make you feel?"

"Makes me feel like I'm not going to give him any more ideas."

So the CEO's first gear behavior triggered a first gear response in the CFO. He would no longer share his ideas. See how that would damage not only the relationship between the two men but also the company.

When he was President of the United States, Harry Truman had a plaque on his desk that read, "All things are possible if you don't care who gets the credit." That's a really enlightened way of thinking, but it goes against what many people are taught in the business world, which is that you have to self-promote if you want to get ahead. You have to speak up for yourself because if you don't, nobody else will.

I asked the CFO to give me another example of his boss's behavior.

"He's a bully. He likes to mock and demean other people. He seems to get a lot of pleasure out of putting people down. If you have an idea, and he doesn't like it, he shames you in front of everyone."

"Okay, he takes credit for your work, he bullies other people, what else?"

"He's sexist."

"Give me an example," I said.

"Some women have said he makes them feel uncomfortable." The CFO looked at me and asked, "What do I do?"

"Well, you work for a guy who's often in first gear. What do you think you should do?"

"I guess it's like a marriage that's going through a very bad patch. I have three choices: I can accept it, I can change it, or I can leave."

I agreed with him and said, "You can try to change it by talking to your boss or to someone in HR and explain your challenges. Or you can accept the situation. But if you do accept it, and you're working for a leader who's in first gear, likely you'll drop back to first gear too."

If the manager or supervisor of a division or department is consistently demonstrating first gear behavior, then that may become the norm for the division. That's why it's so crucial for leaders to become role models of the behavior they want to see in their employees. They really do have to 'walk the walk and talk the talk'.

Roger Eacock was that kind of CEO. "When I ran a company, I remember walking down onto the plant floor and talking to some of our workers. These people may not have worn a suit to work, but don't kid yourself, they were very smart people. I'd ask them for their ideas on how to make things better and they would look shocked. Shocked, because no one in management had ever bothered to solicit their opinion before. Often we would end up implementing some of their ideas, and it was great to see the pride they exhibited when they knew they were part of making a difference."

Chapter 3

Second Gear Behavior

"Much of human behavior can be explained and predicted as a response to incentives."

Robert Sexton, 'Exploring Economics'

Second gear behavior is all about doing something in the expectation of receiving a reward.

How does a driver in second gear act? He or she will give way to another car but will then wait to receive an acknowledgment from the other driver. Typically, this will be a 'thank you' wave.

Here's the problem: if the driver doesn't get any acknowledgment, he or she will most likely revert to first gear.

"So that's all the thanks I get! Well, that's the last car I let in."

And that's often how a silo gets created: "Well, that's the last time I let *a BMW* in!"

The workplace operates on incentive systems, with rewards for good behavior and punishments for poor behavior. This is the 'carrot and stick' system, and it works to a certain degree.

It's why so many companies offer incentive systems. "Do this, and you get Employee of the Month." "Do this, and you'll get gift certificates or cash bonuses."

There are many problems with incentives of any kind. For a start, they can create entitlement and expectations.

My wife told me about a performance review she once did in which she gave a young manager a good but not great rating.

At the end of the meeting, he said, "But look, I come to work, and I do a really good job." She said to him, "It's *your job* to do really good work. That's what you get a salary for." So although second gear works well, it can create an expectation of reward.

There's also the danger that the desired behavior will only manifest when there's a chance of a reward and disappear when the reward is removed.

"Research suggests that by and large, rewards succeed at securing one thing only: temporary compliance," writes Alfie Kohn in the *'Harvard Business Review'*.[17] "When it comes to producing lasting change in attitudes and behavior, however, rewards, like punishment, are strikingly ineffective. Once the rewards run out, people revert to their old behaviors."

So why do most executives continue to rely on incentive programs?

---

[17] *'Why Incentive Plans Cannot Work'*, Kohn, Alfie, *Harvard Business Review* (Sep-Oct issue), www.hbr.org, Sep-Oct 1993

"Perhaps it's because few people take the time to examine the connection between incentive programs and problems with workplace productivity and morale," says Kohn. "Rewards buy temporary compliance, so it looks like the problems are solved. It's harder to spot the harm they cause over the long term."

Withdrawing or withholding an incentive program can be perceived as a punishment, and in that sense, it can be more demoralizing than if nothing had been offered in the first place. The more desirable the reward that is being offered, the greater the sense of disappointment when it's withdrawn or withheld.

This happened at a bank where my wife once worked. It had an incentive program where if you helped somebody else he or she gave you a little checkmark, and you got a point. Once you'd accumulated a certain number of points, you could redeem them for gift certificates or products. So the more good deeds you did, the more points you received.

But one year, the bank's sales were down, and it was forced to pull back on the reward system. The problem was people had become so accustomed to being rewarded for good behavior that they'd demand, "Well, where's my point?" when they did something they regarded as being worthy of a reward. Not getting rewarded caused a lot of resentment amongst employees. Within a short space of time, the helpful behavior began to decline.

Then there's the danger that the incentive system actually rewards the wrong behavior. In his hugely popular management article, 'On the folly of rewarding A, while hoping for B' Steven Kerr wrote, "Managers who complain about lack of motivation in their workers might do well to consider the possibility that the reward systems they have installed are paying off for behavior other than what they are seeking.[1818]

"A first step for such managers might be to explore what types of behavior are currently being rewarded," he said.

"Chances are excellent that these managers will be surprised by what they find—that their firms are not rewarding what they assume they are. In fact, such undesirable behavior by organizational members as they have observed may be explained largely by the reward systems in use."

Management consultant and author Dave Logan has come to the same conclusion.[19] After spending much of his life studying—both as an academic and a consultant—how companies use incentives, he believes that the majority of companies mess this issue up. The result is confusion, frustration and often, the opposite of what they intended.

He says they get it horribly wrong in four ways:

1. They incentivize employees to do things they feel they can't do.

"I've been in hundreds of meetings over the years when an executive will stand up and announce, with excitement in his or her voice, that the incentive paid to salespeople will double for each new customer they bring in," says Logan. The announcement is often met with astonishment and dismay. That's because the salespeople are already doing their best but customers just aren't buying.

---

[18] 'On the folly of rewarding A, while hoping for B', The Academy of Management Executive, Kerr, Steven, Feb 1995
[19] *'How employee incentives can backfire'*, Logan, Dave, MoneyWatch, CBS News, www.cbsnews.com, Feb 15, 2012

Instead of finding out why people aren't buying the products or services, executives try to incentivize salespeople. The salespeople, in turn, feel pressured. So although the company's goal is to boost sales, the salespeople's goal becomes to find new jobs in a less pressurized environment.

2. They address a problem involving just a few employees through a new incentive system that everyone has to follow.

Logan gives the example of a company where one department was abusing the work-from-home privilege, so the head of human resources announced that workers in that department had to keep track of their days at home, and this record had to be signed by the employee's supervisor. If the number of days at home exceeded a threshold, the offenders would not receive a performance bonus.

"Everyone knew the problem was about a small group—maybe four people out of over 100," recalls Logan. "Rather than go to the offenders, management instead instituted new rules that added paperwork and bureaucracy for everyone."

This not only made management seem out of touch but drew people's attention to the fact they could work from home if they wanted. Seeing it as a perk, employees worked from home much more. So instead of increasing the time employees spent in the office—which was the goal of the incentive program—the result was a decrease in the time they spent in the office and overall performance.

3. They incentivize workers to do things they believe violates their values.

This is often seen in group medical practices where doctors are rewarded for seeing more patients. While the goal of increased productivity is necessary, it often results in the opposite, reports Logan.

"The way the plan is implemented in many companies sends the message that doctors won't, unless bribed, do their best," he says. This is offensive to doctors.

"Over time, many see the incentive as a signal that they should spend less time per patient, which means not practicing good medicine.

"As the doctors talk, someone will point out that they see the maximum number of patients while maintaining professional ethics. The money they leave on the table is a "tax for doing the right thing." It comes across as honorable to do less, with doctors high-fiving each other for seeing fewer patients."

4. They announce a new strategy in the form of a new incentive plan.

Logan gives the example of a company that announced any new projects done for Asian-based companies would result in a bonus for sales staff and technical workers. It went down like a brick because many employees had chosen to work for the company because they wouldn't have to travel internationally.

"Many had small children and didn't want to be away for days or weeks at a time," says Logan. So while the goal of the incentive program was to increase the company's Asian client base, it resulted in no increase in the Asian client base and low motivation among the sales staff.

"In every one of these situations, the problem wasn't the incentive itself; it was the way the incentive was implemented.

"It was heavy-handed, unilateral, and came as a surprise," he says.

Srikanth Srinivas, the author of 'Shocking Velocity', described in the Harvard Business Review his experience of an incentive system that had obviously backfired.[20] It happened when he was in an Asian city and had to visit a client at a factory quite far from his city center hotel. The client suggested he get a bus and gave him directions to the nearest bus stop.

"I went to the bus stop and waited. Several buses came close to the stop, but they all whizzed by without stopping. It wasn't that the buses were full. In fact, there were plenty of empty seats. After half a dozen buses came tantalizingly close but without stopping to pick up passengers, I finally caught a cab."

He arrived late to the meeting and apologized to the client before explaining the cause of his delay.

"The client laughed and said, 'The driver's bonus depends on whether or not he reaches his destination on time. So during peak traffic when they find they are running behind, they don't bother picking up passengers!'

"Here was the height of insanity—an incentive system that succeeded only in defeating its original purpose. At peak time, exactly when more passengers need to be picked up, it was better for the driver to go empty. Frustrated citizens, lost revenue and increased costs all thanks to the incentive system and the driver's desire to maximize his individual gain. Further, every 'man on the street' seemed to know the problem, but not the organization that ran the buses. Or, equally baffling, they knew it and chose to ignore it."

---

[20] 'When Your Incentive System Backfires', Srinivas Srikanth, Govindarajan Vijay, Harvard Business Review, www.hbr.org, Feb 21, 2013

There's another problem with incentives, and it's that people have a remarkable capacity to play the system. Here's a perfect example.

Back when Vietnam was under French colonial rule, the regime in Hanoi wanted to rid the place of rats.[21] To do that, it launched a bounty program that paid a reward for each rat that was killed.

To obtain the bounty, individuals had to provide a severed rat tail as evidence they'd killed a rat.

Some time later, colonial officials began noticing more and more tailless rats in Hanoi. An investigation revealed why: the Vietnamese rat catchers would capture rats, cut off their tails, and then release them back into the sewers so they could breed and produce more rats. The rat catchers could then get even more rewards.

It can work like that in the workplace too with employees doing just enough to qualify for a reward but nothing more. They will do the bare minimum they can get away with.

During university, I took a summer job with a unionized company. On my first day, I walked onto the lot and started picking up trash.

An older employee came up to me and asked me what I was doing.

"I'm new here, and I'm just picking up trash," I told him.

"Yeah, well stop working so hard," he replied, "You're making the rest of us look bad."

---

[21] *'Of Rats, Rice, and Race: The Great Hanoi Rat Massacre, an Episode in French Colonial History'*, Vann, Michael G., French Colonial History 4, 2003

When one of my nephews was about 16 years old, he got his first real paying job. It was a part-time position at a unionized company, which meant he had to pay union fees.

Now, being 16, he was pretty excited about getting his first payment. But that excitement gave way to fury when he saw his pay was much less than he'd expected because taxes and union fees had been subtracted.

He decided to read the union handbook closely, and that's where he discovered that under union rules, employees were allowed to arrive at work no more than nine minutes late and leave work no more than nine minutes early.

He told his Mom that from then on he was going to arrive at work exactly nine minutes late and leave work exactly nine minutes early every day.

He was operating in second gear. He was behaving very rationally according to his incentive system but following the *letter* of the law rather than the *spirit* of the law.

What advice could we give him?

Perhaps to advise him that one day he will be looking for another job and will need references. What does he want his references to say? That he's a guy who only does what's in his job description but not one thing more? Or does he want them to say 'this guy went above and beyond'? That he's a good guy, and he chipped in to help even though it wasn't part of his job and that he thought of the bigger picture, of the company's best interests?

In companies, people behave according to the incentive system they have. When the company has different incentive systems, problems can occur.

For example, I spent six months working with Nicolas Heldmann and his Accounting Services division at OpenText, Canada's largest software company. One day we were discussing the challenges his team experienced with other divisions in the company.

"Finance obviously has to review the credit ratings of prospective clients before the salespeople can take orders and ship product," one team member said. "Sometimes the salespeople call us at the last minute. We have a process, but the salespeople always want us to bend the rules and get things under the wire."

I asked them if any of them had ever worked in Sales. None of them had, so I explained that incentive systems are different in Sales than they are in Finance. Most people in Finance get a two-week paycheck, and if there's a bonus or profit sharing structure in the company, they'll get a little more.

In Sales, the system is different. The compensation is usually tied to the behavior of the prospect or customer. Sales is a company's revenue realizer, so salespeople need the clients to buy. They will also do what they can to make sure they get that purchase order before the quarter is over so they can get their bonus. If that means calling on people in the Finance or Accounts team and trying to persuade them to push the process so the sales can be made before the deadline, then so be it.

Their behavior is entirely logical, but it's based on how the clients are acting or how their bonus is structured.

Sometimes, there needs to be a compromise. For example, when I worked in sales, I'd often be out in the field and when I returned I'd have to submit my expense reports. One day, I received a missive from Finance saying the process for submitting expenses had changed.

The new process involved filling out a long and complicated document. It created five times the amount of work for me. I was pretty upset because, for me, time was money. I had to be out there generating revenue, not sitting at my desk working on a spreadsheet.

So I called the Finance Department and explained my objections to the new system. The head of the Finance Department said, "We really have a problem with the old process. It wasn't constructive."

The bottom line was the old system inconvenienced the finance department, and the new system inconvenienced the sales staff, so we had to find a middle ground.

There are three ways to get over a barrier like this.

The first is for both parties to explain the company incentive system within which they're operating. The idea is to get both sides to understand how the other side is incentivized.

The people who usually have the greatest empathy in a company are those who work in more than one function or division. Sometimes, understanding actually only comes from walking a mile in someone else's shoes.

A woman I spoke with recently told me she'd spent six months working in every division of an international cosmetics company before assuming the finance role for which she'd been employed. During the six months, she worked in every one of the company's departments from Distribution to Marketing. She packed boxes of cosmetics, learned how to give facials in department stores, and helped the Marketing Department organize press conferences. By the time she started her job, she not only understood how the company worked but also had tremendous empathy with employees in each department.

So that's one way. Another way is to encourage all employees to think of the company's vision. Most people function very rationally according to what's good for themselves or for their tribe. In a business setting, their tribe is most likely to be their department or division. They need to think of the bigger picture.

For this to happen, the company needs to have a culture of transparency. I remember when Steve Malinowski, President and CEO of the Kraus Group, got up to address his entire company. He said, "I'm going to give you more information than most CEOs will ever give you. Some of what I'm about to tell you is confidential, but I'm going to share it with you because I want you to be involved in the broader vision of the company. It's about where we're going and where we want to be as a company.

"But I need something from you in return. I need to be able to trust you. I need your assurance that you will not go home and tell this story to our competitors or industry partners."

People were astonished that their CEO was being so transparent. Later, I asked him why he did it. He said, "I've found that transparency works really well. The more transparent you are with your employees, the better they understand the bigger picture of what we are trying to achieve, and the better they adapt their activities to fit it."

So getting employees to understand the company's vision helps too.

The third way is to encourage employees to consider the best interests of the end-user. What's in the best interests of the person who buys our products or services?

I was once asked to talk to the professors and administration staff at a major Canadian university. We were talking about silos because you often get silos in universities between the professors and administration staff.

The head of the Finance Division recalled how a professor had come to him and demanded a new photocopier. He was very adamant about it. The one he wanted had more functions than the one in his office.

The division head looked at him and said, "You'll get a new photocopier when you explain to me how this will benefit the students at the university."

The professor had to go away and think how the photocopier would help the students who were paying for their tuition.

Every division in a company has priorities, but those should take a back seat to the needs of the end-user, which is the customer or client. You need your employees to work together to make sure the customer is really overjoyed with the quality of the product or service he or she is getting from your company. When that happens, every division will be rewarded because revenues will skyrocket.

It's what Kelly Kloss, City Manager of Fort Saskatchewan, did to encourage his employees to move from second to third gear.

"We are essentially operating 15 different businesses. People were really aligned with their group but to be truly successful we needed to all come together as one," he recalls.

"Establishing a Team Fort Sask philosophy helped staff to understand we are really one company with many parts. Each must do their part, so the whole organization is successful in achieving our vision of 'Engaged People, Thriving Community'.

"Our goal is to deliver what I call the 'Wow Factor' to everyone we come in contact with. Each staff is a window into our organization, or one could say our 'best advertiser' of the great community we live in.

"Utilizing real opportunities to weave this philosophy throughout the organization helped to us move forward. For example, when our Parks department cut down a huge hedge adjacent to one of our main parks, they did not realize the ownership our residents had in what was happening.

"There was community reaction mostly because of the lack of information as to how the work would revitalize the hedge so it could grow back healthier. So when it came time to take down the second hedge, Parks contacted our Communications Department so the message of why got out to the public, and they made sure our Council members and all staff were informed in case they received questions."

Chapter 4

Third Gear Behavior

"How selfish soever man may be supposed there are evidently some principles in his nature, which interest him in the fortune of others, and render their happiness necessary to him, though he derives nothing from it, except the pleasure of seeing it."

Adam Smith, 'The Theory of Moral Sentiments'

A few years ago, I was on my way to the airport after giving a lecture in the Canadian prairies. It was in February, and it was extremely cold—easily minus 30 degrees.

On the way, I stopped the car to take a photograph because the scenery was quite beautiful.

So there I was by the side of my car on this lonely highway when I saw a car approaching in the distance. As it drew nearer, it began to slow down. I was thinking, "Oh my God, serial killer!"

The car drew up beside me, and the driver lowered the window and said, "Are you okay?

Collecting myself, I replied, "Yeah. I'm just taking a picture. I used to live here when I was younger."

"Oh, okay," the driver said then raised the window and drove off.

Later, when I got to the airport, I spoke about the encounter on the highway with a businessman I met. I told him I was kind of surprised. Nothing like that would happen in Toronto, I said.

The businessman said, "But it's minus 30 degrees and that guy was worried your car had broken down and just wanted to make sure you were okay. He was probably a local guy so he knows you could die out there if your car was broken down. You'd freeze to death. He was just seeing that you were okay."

The stranger on the highway was demonstrating third gear behavior. He didn't offer help in the expectation of being rewarded. He did it because he obviously believed it was the right thing to do.

The businessman then commented, "I bet this wouldn't happen in Toronto, though. People in big cities don't help each other."

I responded "Not on a major highway, but that's not because people don't want to help. It's because if a car breaks down, help is usually immediately available. It's also dangerous to get out of a car while hundreds of vehicles are racing by on the road. So the incentives in larger cities are different, but that doesn't mean everyone is in first gear."

Third gear behavior is governed by intrinsic reward. A lawyer once told me it should be called 'dispositional attribution' because it's a state of mind that is independent of other states of mind.

A driver in third gear will allow another driver to get ahead of him and not expect any kind of acknowledgment.

Here's a very simple example of third gear in practice: someone walks by your desk in the morning and says "Good morning." You return the greeting. A little while later, you get in the elevator in your office building, and you say "Good morning" to the person who's standing there. The other person doesn't return your greeting. You get absolutely no response. If you're in third gear, you don't mind.

The way most people react to a situation like this is to feel disgruntled because they didn't get the expected response; they didn't get the reward. It's then that they're likely to start judging the other person.

"Huh, what a jerk!"

"He thinks he's better than me."

"Arrogant jerk."

"Snob."

These responses are second gear: *"I did something nice, but I didn't get a reward. That's not fair!"*

A third gear mindset is different. It's not judgmental. It might be curious, but not judgmental. In third gear, you do something because it's the right thing to do and that's who you are. You don't do something because you expect a response in return.

You are trying to be a 'good guy' or an 'amazing woman', and you treat everyone you meet as a real human being and with respect. I was inspired to call this approach 'RHB' after hearing the following story from Adi Treasurywala, a specialist in the field of life sciences technology commercialization, and now president of business development consultancy Arrowcan Partners.

Adi told me that when he attended events, he usually asked that only his first name be used on his nametag, instead of his last name and credentials (PhD, BSc.). He did it, he said, because it eliminated much of the generalization and stereotyping that occurred when people saw a foreign name or noticed a lot of credentials. It felt more authentic and allowed him to connect with people as real human beings.

He was once invited to attend a prestigious medical conference in Boston and the conference organizer requested his professional credentials for his nametag. Adi asked that they list his first name only.

The conference organizer said medical conference attendees tended to gravitate towards those who shared similar degrees and titles and therefore first and last name and professional credentials were mandatory.

So Adi asked that his nametag read: "Adi Treasurywala, PhD, BSc, RHB."

At the gala dinner, the company's president stopped by Adi's table and seeing his nametag, asked him about 'RHB'. Adi told him it meant 'Real Human Being'.

The nametag was a hit as the president started introducing him to other participants as "This is Dr. Adi Treasurywala, he's an RHB you know!"

I began to share Adi's story in my talks. One day, a woman approached me after one such talk and asked if I would present the keynote address at her company's upcoming conference. "In our company, Sales hate Marketing, Marketing hate Finance, Finance hate IT, and everyone hates head office. We need to have more RHBs in our company" she commented.

To think like an RHB, you need to do more than respect your fellow human beings, however. You need to focus on developing a reputation based on intrinsic reward.

In 2003, I met Dr. Graham Smith, one of the founders of CanBioPharma Consulting Inc., which provides consultative support to clients regarding the nonclinical development of therapeutic drugs and biologics, and medical devices, as well as risk assessment of environmental chemicals.

I asked Graham what kind of reputation he would like for CanBioPharma. He replied, "I want them to say 'They're good guys, and you can trust them.'"

Notice that Graham did not mention his product or service. He used the phrase 'good guy'.

In every language, there is a word or a phrase for someone we trust enough to send people to when they have problems.

"Call Steve; he's a good guy." "Call Barbara; she's amazing."

I have accumulated about 25 translations of 'good guy' or 'amazing woman' from around the world. They all mean "If you have a problem, you should go see this person: they can help you. Use my name; tell them I sent you."

Why do people refer someone to their associates? They do it because they know the person they refer will provide friends or colleagues with reliable, quality, personable and timely advice.

The Gold Standard of Reputation

There are four key elements of being a good guy or an amazing woman.

1. Knowledge, experience, and skill

You have knowledge, skill and experience and willingly share them with others. Your coworkers and employees come to you for assistance because they know you will whenever possible give them the advice or support they need.

2. Personality

Knowledge isn't the only element in reputation. We all know very smart people who sometimes find it difficult to relate to others. You need to have the personality to get along with others.

It means you try to adapt to others rather than expect they will always adapt to your personality.

3. Reliability

You need to keep your promises so that you are known for being trustworthy.

4. Empathy

Genuinely good people think about others as well as themselves. They participate in charity drives. They spend a few minutes taking questions from a student. Companies call this corporate responsibility.

The Rule of Reputation

The rule of reputation is simple: it has to be earned. You need to consistently do quality work, get along with co-workers, be reliable, and have some empathy.

People in third gear do good work whether they get a daily pat on the back or not. When you take the time to thank them, you will often get the response: "I was just doing my job."

Someone with a 'good guy' or 'amazing woman' reputation is more likely to be asked for advice and help by colleagues and friends. He or she is also more likely to be noticed by employers, attract new clients and sales through word-of-mouth, and to be admired within his or her company and local community.

What do people in third gear want? They really only want one thing: they want to be around other people in third gear.

In every company, third gear people form networks and refer to each other as good guys and amazing women. *They do this because they know these people have earned their trust, and they will make them look good.*

Interestingly, a study by Google has shown that the best-performing teams are those in which the members respect one another's emotions and are mindful that all members should contribute to the conversation equally.[22] Their success, Google's Project Aristotle researchers discovered, has less to do with who is in a team, and more with how team members interact with one another.

---

[22] 'After years of intensive analysis, Google discovers the key to good teamwork is being nice', Mohdin, Aamna, Feb 26, 2016, www.qz.com

Project Aristotle involved interviews with hundreds of Google employees and analysis of data about the people in more than 100 teams at the company. It lasted more than three years.

It found that team success relies on 'psychological safety', a model of teamwork in which members have a shared belief that it is safe to take risks and share a range of ideas without the fear of being humiliated. Harvard Business School professor Amy Edmondson wrote in a study published in 1999 that psychological safety is "a sense of confidence that the team will not embarrass, reject, or punish someone for speaking up.[23] It's a shared belief held by members of a team that the team is safe for interpersonal risk-taking.

"It describes a team climate characterized by interpersonal trust and mutual respect in which people are comfortable being themselves," she said.

This proves, once again, that encouraging employees to behave in third gear also boosts collaboration and productivity.

---

[23] *'What Google Learned From Its Quest to Build the Perfect Team'*, Duhigg, Charles, New York Times magazine, Feb 25, 2016, www.nyt.com

Lead by example

"Great leaders are almost always great simplifiers."

Colin Powell

Most people who are top achievers in companies have some sort of inner code that they live by. It might have come from their parents, teachers, religion, friends, or even fictional characters. It may even be inspired by their favorite superhero. What matters is the code is like a moral or ethical compass that guides them.

What I'm talking about here are people who are characterized as good guys and amazing women. They're the inspiring leaders.

The former President and CEO of San Antonio-based Sirius Computer Solutions and philanthropist, Harvey Najim, was one such leader.

His father, the co-owner of a wholesale candy, syrup and tobacco business, instilled in him a strong moral and work ethic.[24] Sometimes his father would bring home invoices for Harvey to work on, while other times he was expected to work in the family business.

"Ever since I was knee-high to a grasshopper, my father often took me to work with him at his wholesale candy, syrup and tobacco business," he told Keith Harrell, author

---

[24] 'For Harvey Najim, life is about 'servant leadership: Charity—for kids, especially—is his passion', Fletcher Stoeltje Melissa, Express News, www.expressnews.com, Sep 10, 2015

of *The Attitude of Leadership: Taking the Lead and Keeping It*.[25]

Harvey and his cousin were given work to do. One day, that was moving 250 four-gallon cases of soda, sweeping underneath them then returning them to their original places.

"I complained, mumbling out loud that the job was a pointless task and not worth doing. My father told me, 'Son, it's important to do the right thing, whether or not it will ever get noticed. If you do the right thing for the right reasons, you will never regret it, and you never know what will happen as a result.'"

Later that afternoon, a health inspector showed up and insisted Harvey's father move the soda cases aside to see if the facilities were thoroughly cleaned.

"Dad did, they were, and I learned a lifelong lesson that I continue to practice in my personal and professional life."

Here's another example of a man who acted according to his own code.

Back in the year 2000, Brigadier General Peter Atkinson was Commanding Officer (CO) of the Royal Canadian Dragoons. Three of his squadrons had been deployed to the Balkans, so that year he flew to Kosovo to inspect one of the three squadrons.[26]

One of the days, General Atkinson spent a day on patrol with his tank unit. Everything proceeded as expected during the morning. But after lunch, things took a turn for the

[25] *The Attitude of Leadership: Taking the Lead and Keeping It*', Harrell, Keith D., John Wiley & Sons, Inc., www.wiley.com, 2003
[26] '*13068 Pete Atkinson: Majored in football and minored in history*', Scilley, Claude, eVeritas, http://everitas.rmcclub.ca, Jan 11, 2015

worse. It was when General Atkinson climbed back into one of the tanks that he noticed something had become dislodged, and dropped down to snap it back into place.

As he did, his helmet caught the rear handle of the machine gun, and it fired off three shots. General Atkinson explains what happened next.

"I looked down the barrel to see where the shots had gone. Fortunately for me, those three shots had gone into the rear of a tank in front of me. Had there been a soldier in front of that gun, he would be dead. In fact, had there been five or six soldiers in front of that gun, they'd all be dead. I was very lucky no one was hurt.

"So I turned myself in to the Commander when we got back in. I told him what happened and went to the NIS, gave them the statement. I knew I would be court-martialed. I actually thought my career was done."

So why did he turn himself in?

"Why did I admit my mistake? That's what leaders do. Leaders lead and take responsibility for their actions. If you make a mistake, you own up to it. I knew, as a CO, that I had to set the example because no matter who you are, you can't only do the right thing when other people are looking. The young second lieutenant who was the troop leader had said, 'Boss, it's just us.'"

In other words, you don't have to say anything because you're going to get into a lot of trouble. "I said to him, 'I'm the CO. I am responsible. I always have to set the example.'"

He was court-martialed and fined $5,000.

The next day, he was about to speak to his troops about the lessons he'd learned from the experience when he got a phone call. "It was the Commander of the Army, General Leach. He said, 'Peter, I understand you're speaking with your soldiers. You set the example that we want out of our leaders. You took responsibility for your mistakes, and I know you took that on the chin, but I just want you to know you did the right thing. Our plan is still to promote you to Colonel and make you the base commander in Kingston. Keep up the good work and good luck.'"

So third gear is doing the right thing even when there's a very real prospect of you getting punished for it.

You have to walk the walk if you're a CEO or President of a company. As Gandhi said, "Be the change that you wish to see in the world." You can't be in first gear and expect your people to be out there in third gear.

An employee in third gear will do an excellent job whether they're managed or not. They're doing it because they want to do a great job. A good guy in Finance has more in common with a good guy in Sales than he does with the rest of his team.

When you're in third gear, you're not a doormat or a pushover. You just operate according to an inner ethical code. I teach people to think of themselves as working *with* a company, not *for* a company. That's an RHB mindset: work *with* people not *for* people. Don't be subservient. Think of yourself as being a partner in the business. It's a really important mindset to have because it's about feeling as if you are in control of your career. You are your own CEO/CFO within a company.

Third gear is asymmetrical. You do something, but you may not get a one-to-one response back.

About a month after I had delivered a keynote address, a woman called me.

> "You've really made a difference in my job. I work in a high-stress industry, and there's a lady on my floor, and she's always asking for help.
>
> "Last Friday afternoon, I had to pick my son up and take him to a football game. My son had said to me that morning, 'Don't be late Mom.' I'd promised him I'd be there on time.
>
> "Anyway, five minutes before four that afternoon, that lady came up to my desk and said she had a couple of questions. I told her that I had to go in five minutes because I had to pick up my son for his game.
>
> "'No problem,' she said. 'It will only take five minutes.'
>
> "It didn't take five minutes. It took twenty minutes. At the end of it, she never even said 'Thank you.'
>
> "I raced home to pick up my son to take him to his game. He was freaking out at me because he was going to be more than ten minutes late for the game.
>
> "Normally, I'd be so angry with that lady. I'd tell my husband about her, and I'd tell my son about her. I'd probably tell a couple of my colleagues about her on Monday morning too. But I knew that would be second gear behavior.
>
> "I'd offered her help because that's who I am and it's the right thing to do. It had been my choice to stay with her for twenty minutes versus five.

"So I shifted to third gear, and I just let that anger and resentment go. My son had a great game, and I forgot about it.

"Guess what happens on Monday? I turn on my computer, and I'm sitting there when that lady comes up to me with a little bouquet of flowers. She puts the bouquet of flowers on my desk and says, 'I just want to thank you. I don't say it often enough to people around here. I really appreciated your help on Friday afternoon, and I'm sorry I made you late'.

"The great thing was not the flowers—although they were lovely—it was that you saved me two days of anger."

Holding onto grudges is a waste of your time and energy. As Confucius once said, "To be wronged is nothing, unless you continue to remember it."

The way to encourage more third gear behavior in others is to demonstrate what third gear is yourself.

Recently, I did a training seminar on customer service for a company. I didn't tell them how to behave in third gear. Instead, I gave them a scenario with a customer and asked them what a first gear, second gear, and third gear response would be. And then we workshopped it.

Workshopping the answers is a really great thing. I taught scuba diving for many years, and I found people learned a skill better if they self-corrected than if you got in their way all the time and corrected them while they were learning the skill.

The real sign of success is when employees start assessing their own behavior in terms of gears. They start using the language and identifying the gears they're behaving in and changing their behavior.

You really want a culture where, if somebody starts dropping back to first gear and acting a certain way, it's not the CEO or management but other employees who say, "Hey that's not what we do around here. That's not what we stand for." One CEO called it 'an employee-owned culture, not a CEO-driven culture'.

When people take pride in where they work, and they like the people they work with, they want to protect it.

Kelly Kloss, the City Manager of Fort Saskatchewan, says he saw this in action recently. "A department here had an extremely hard time at budget and a number of people from other departments went down there to say to the people in that department things like, 'How are you doing? Is there anything we can do to help? We're here to offer moral support for you if you need to talk.'"

Part of role modeling is treating people as human beings, not as commodities or widgets or cogs in a machine. Silos happen in a company sometimes because people don't feel respected.

I heard a speaker at a conference who'd been to Harvard Business School for his MBA. He recalled a time when he and his classmates were asked by a visiting Professor if they knew the name of the custodian who cleaned the room. Nobody did. The Professor said, "Let me tell you, your success as a CEO will come from you knowing the name of that custodian."

Harvey Najim says he took the time to learn the name of each of his employees.[27] Before selling his shares in Sirius Computer Solutions, he told Keith Harrell, author of *'The Attitude of Leadership: Taking the Lead and Keeping It'*, "I may be the sole shareholder in my company, but I'm clear that if employees are to have a stake in the success of Sirius, they have to know every day that their efforts are acknowledged and appreciated.

"It's not just important for a leader to genuinely care about the people in an organization. For employees to know it, you've got to show it."

So once or twice a day, he would walk around and talk with people throughout the company.

"I'll ask how they're doing and what they're working on," he said. "I pass on compliments from their supervisors. I make it a point to know the name of everyone who works for me." He'd also know when their work anniversaries were, whether they were married and had kids, and even whether they'd just got back from surgery.

"People don't care how much you know until they know how much you care. My interest is genuine, and it pays dividends... We may be high-tech, but we're also high-touch, in that we stay connected with each other through frequent communication and contact."

Part of getting people to think about third gear is getting them to be aware of what gear they're in.

Kelly Kloss says that when employees, managers or even members of Council come to him with a complaint, he asks them, "Are you trying to make things better or are you

[27] *'The Attitude of Leadership: Taking the Lead and Keeping It'*, Harrell, Keith D., John Wiley & Sons, Inc., www.wiley.com, 2003

trying to blame someone? I know what may be easier at first, but why don't we try to make things better?

"Stop the emails, stop the messages, go over and talk to that person. If you have a problem with people, meet with them and ask, 'how can we work this out?'"

Being asked the question forces people to elevate their thinking.

Chapter 5

The RHB Code

*"It is always easier—and usually far more effective—
to focus on changing your behavior than on changing
the behavior of others."*

Bob Nelson

Two departments were at each other's throats. As you can imagine, the tension between the two was creating all kinds of problems for their organization. I was asked to go in and mediate between the warring factions.

On the morning of the meeting, employees from the two departments were gathered together in a big conference room.

I began by introducing the Real Human Being (RHB) philosophy and the three gears. I explained that it helps break down the barriers between people, and then I wrote the RHB code on the whiteboard.

That is:

- Assume everyone's intelligent
- Have a passion for what you do
- Get over yourself

When I finished, I stood back and told the group, "This is how you stay in third gear. And this is going to be the code of behavior we follow in this meeting today, so let's look at it in a little detail, so you understand how it works.

"First, assume everyone is intelligent." At that, some people in the room laughed while others crossed their arms defensively.

I went on, "What does that mean to all of us here today? As Aristotle once said, 'The mark of an educated mind is you can entertain an idea without accepting it.'

"In other words, we can assume people are intelligent, but we don't need to agree with them or even support them.

"We treat each other with mutual respect. The things that make a meeting go downhill fast are sweeping generalizations and personal insults. The code means you can say 'Bob, I disagree with your idea' but you can't say, 'Bob, you're a moron.'

"Assuming everyone is intelligent also means we don't ascribe behavior to an entire department or division. So we don't say 'Bob, you're a moron just like everyone else over there in the Sales Department.'

More laughter.

"'*Assume everyone is intelligent*' doesn't mean assume everyone's a good guy, and it doesn't mean assume everyone has your best interests at heart. It just means do not pre-judge people and give them credit for having a brain."

There are many benefits to assuming everyone is intelligent.

I used to work with a company that hosted counterterrorism conferences, and we once had a US Naval Intelligence Officer come and speak. He'd worked undercover in al-Qaeda, and a key part of his message that day was, "You better respect the people in al-Qaeda."

A lot of people in the audience weren't happy about that part of his message, I can tell you.

But he went on to say, "They respect you. You don't have to like people to respect them. If you don't respect them, however, you're going to underestimate them. As soon as you underestimate them, they're going to beat you."

I thought that was a really powerful phrase. You might not like the people in another company because they're taking away your market share, but you'd better respect them. If you don't respect them, you'll underestimate them, and when that happens, they'll beat you.

When I worked in sales, I used to take part in a lot of trade shows. I found that as soon as the trade show got quiet, many people would stay seated at their booths and chat with their company colleagues. The rest of us would walk up and down and talk to the people at other booths.

Why did we do it? It's another example of assuming everyone is intelligent. We just never knew who we might meet and what business opportunities we might find. After all, often people on the other booths would be selling to the same type of customers we were. Quite often, they had clients we wouldn't have even heard about. If they liked and trusted us enough, that conversation would turn into a business opportunity.

It also made what could have been a dull couple of hours a heck of a lot more interesting!

Here's another example of the benefits of assuming everyone is intelligent. A while back I was chatting with a receptionist while I waited to see one of the company's executives. She told me she'd worked at the company for seven years.

"Do you enjoy the job?" I asked.

She said she really enjoyed it and how much she admired the company's president. "He's a really remarkable man," she added.

I asked her if she'd ever had anyone treat her as less than intelligent and she said, "A couple of months ago, a guy came in for a job interview here. I took his coat and gave him a glass of water, and he went in to speak to the President.

"An hour later he left and the President came out of his office and said to me, 'So what do you think? Shall we hire him?'

"I said I wouldn't.

"He asked me why not. And I said, 'Because when he called initially, he was very short and rude to me. He was the same way today when I took his coat and got him a glass of water.'"

"'Really? That's strange because he was really charming and forthcoming in the interview.'"

The job applicant had made the mistake of not assuming the receptionist was intelligent. What he couldn't have known was that the president would take the time to check how he had behaved with other employees. He wasn't hired, because the president realized his treatment of the receptionist was indicative of how he'd treat those in the company he considered to be beneath him in importance.

It just shows that your reputation is determined by how you behave when you don't realize you're being observed.

That's what I explained to the people in that mediation meeting. I then told them about the second part of the code, 'Have passion for what you do'.

"In this case," I said, "it means to have a passion for your viewpoint or your opinion." In a situation like that, people can be reluctant to put their ideas forward because they think they're 'stupid' or not worthy of recognition. Or they think they're going to be shouted down by the people who don't agree with what they say.

So I said, "Own your opinion. Say it with confidence. You have a right to be heard."

I asked them to raise their hands if they hated when people replied to the question "How's it going?" with a 45-minute rant about how awful things are in the company. Everyone laughed then and raised their hands. No one it seemed enjoyed listening to a diatribe from someone who'd lost interest in their job or company.

I explained that my background was sales, and the part of my job I loved the most was walking into a room and meeting people and making bridges. It made me a very good salesperson because I loved making those connections and turning them into something long-term. Actually, it's something I still love to do!

I asked, "Who likes doing that too?" and a bunch of people put up their hands. Not surprisingly, the majority who did were salespeople. It's an attribute that will make you an excellent salesperson.

I asked one guy who hadn't put up his hand what his passion was, and he replied, "Entering data." There was quite a bit of laughter in the room at that point—I don't think many people had ever equated data entry with passion before.

He continued, "I like creating order out of chaos. It just makes me really happy when I take all this data and make it really neat and orderly."

I moved around the room asking people what their passion was. Everybody, it seemed, had at least one thing they really loved.

It's really important to let other people know about your passions. They don't always have to be directly related to your job. For instance, a couple of years ago, I was speaking to a woman about doing a keynote address for her company. We were sitting in her office, and I noticed that she didn't have a single photo on her desk or on her walls. It was completely sterile. There was nothing in there that told me who she was as a person. That struck me as a little odd, because generally in an office you'll see one or two photos on a desk or on a wall.

After a few minutes, I asked her why she didn't have any photos of herself or her family anywhere.

She told me it was because she didn't like clutter, particularly in her workspace. "I think it looks unprofessional," she added.

As we talked some more, it became apparent that one of her biggest challenges was that although she was a very high achiever, she had trouble getting people to open up or share information with her.

"Do you think you might seem intimidating to some of your colleagues?" I asked. "That's part of my challenge: getting people to talk and open up to me," she admitted.

I asked her what she did for fun on the weekends or in her spare time, and she told me some of the things she did, including running marathons.

"Well, why don't you bring in a couple of your marathon medals and hang them in the office?" She looked startled. "Why? That's got nothing to do with business."

"Actually, it does. You're treating everyone like you want to be treated. Most people aren't like you. If you're challenged and you want to make connections, you've got to show them what your passions are."

I wasn't sure when I left that she'd act on my suggestion, but she did. We touched base a few weeks after that, and she said, "You're absolutely right. People walked into my office and saw the medals and started asking me about doing marathons.

"Dave, they looked at me like I was a human being rather than their boss."

Remember, if you're in a position of power, you are an intimidating figure to many people. You've got to show your human side to them. Really successful leaders in business will often have something in their office which reveals what their passion is. It might be golf trophies or photos of them doing volunteer work or driving racing cars. It allows them to show they're a human being as well as being in a powerful position within the company.

It even works in job interviews. A friend told me about a job interview he'd been to many years ago. He said it didn't go well. In fact, he was convinced after the third question that the chances of him getting the job were slim.

At the point the hiring manager started to say 'Thank you very much' my friend looked up and saw a framed photo of a sailboat.

"Is that your sailboat?" he asked.

The hiring manager said it was.

"Oh, I've sailed a whole bunch of times."

The interview segued into an intense discussion about sailing. At the end of the conversation, my friend was offered a six-month position in the company as long as he agreed to go out and crew the hiring manager's sailboat on weekends.

He ended up working for that company for 25 years and retired as a vice president. This proves that revealing the things you're passionate about and showing your humanity can help you to connect with other people. When that happens, the barriers come down.

The people in the mediation meeting were nodding their heads at that point. I then explained the third part of the code, 'Get over yourself'.

"For this meeting, 'Get over yourself' means staying open to new ideas. It means not clinging to your way of doing things just because 'it's the way they've always been done around here.' If new evidence comes to the table from someone, accept it. Let that person know. Say, 'You know, you're right. You've changed my mind. Let's go your route.'

That's not a sign of weakness—it's a sign of strength, of self-confidence, and self-assuredness."

By the end of that meeting, the two departments had reached agreement on the most contentious issues. Following the code by respecting one another meant the way had been cleared for a discussion about how they could work together.

The key to knocking down silos and barriers is getting people to treat each other as human beings. When they stop treating people as being different from them or part of another tribe (such as 'Sales' or 'Men' or 'Millennials'), they open the way for real communication.

The Three Cs: Using the RHB code

In my seminars, I give people practical tools that they can use immediately to overcome silos of any kind. For example, I suggest that whenever they meet someone, they give that person a *compliment*, look for a *commonality* (a shared passion or interest), and then ask that person what their greatest *challenge* is.

The *compliment* is based on part one of the code: assume everyone is intelligent.

The *commonality* is based on the second part of the code: have passion for what you do. Just getting people to seek out commonalities goes a long way to knocking down silos. When they find they have even one passion or interest in common, they are less likely to regard each other as being different or 'not in my tribe'.

When people realize they have shared passions or interests, the 'Us versus Them' thinking starts to disappear. You'll get two people who would usually go head to head realizing they both love supporting the New York Knicks—suddenly, they have a shared passion.

"That guy in Admin has a kid in Scouts too, so he can't be all that bad."

"She's 20 years older than me, but she's got a kid in pre-school too, so she knows how hard it is to be a working Mom."

"Can't wait to find out what that guy in Marketing thought of the game."

The **challenge** is based on the third part of the code: Get over yourself. I always remind people that *'get over yourself'* is meant as a whisper to yourself, not as a directive to other people. It's about telling yourself that yours is not the only way. You need to listen to other people.

Dr. Phil was once doing a counseling session with someone who was having problems with work colleagues and said to her, "When you have problems with people, you have to ask yourself, 'Is it an intent, or is it impact?'"

The woman asked him to explain.

He replied, "You're getting upset because of what they're doing, aren't you?"

"Yes."

"Did they wake up that morning and intend to upset you by doing it that way?"

"No, I guess not."

"It's an impact issue then. It's nothing personal, right?"

"Yeah, I guess it was."

"If you examine every problem you have you'll find that 98-99% of them are impact problems, not intent problems."

Hardly anyone wakes up thinking, "Today is the day I'm going to make that person's life a living Hell."

The point of getting over yourself is that when you do, you're in a position where you can make a real connection with another person. It means considering someone else's needs and issues rather than your own. A simple way to do that is to ask the other person what their biggest challenge is.

A couple of years ago I did a keynote address at a bank. A little while later, I got a call from a woman who had been in the audience. She told me she would often have disagreements with a woman from the company's Australian division.

"We never saw eye to eye," she said, before blurting out, "I really didn't like her. But then you came and gave your talk. You said to turn around and ask the person sitting behind you 'What's your biggest challenge?' Well, I did that and, oh God, she was the one sitting behind me. I kind of winced when I realized it was her, but I asked the question anyway.

"The other woman said, 'Right now, it's my six-year-old daughter—she has autism, and we're trying to get her into a school. I'm really frustrated about the lack of good programs for children with autism'.

"I told her my 16-year-old daughter has autism too, and that's exactly the problem we've struggled with for the past ten years. I said, 'I can give you some resources and some links.'

"Dave, my relationship with that woman has totally changed. I realized that a lot of the behavior she was bringing to the office was stress-related because of her daughter."

People might be grappling with all kinds of non-work related issues. They might be looking after aging parents, or have kids with medical problems. They might be going through a particularly bad patch with their spouse or children. Sometimes those things manifest in their behavior at work. You won't know that until you ask the question, "What's your biggest challenge right now?"

There's an element of humanity in RHB: we can be successful in business, but we can also be human beings as well.

A common silo at work is the perceived 'gap' between different generations. Here's some fascinating research that shows people of all ages value the same things but just express them differently.

After analyzing seven years of research from people of different generations, Jennifer Deal from the Center for Creative Leadership and author of 'Retiring the Generation Gap: How Employees Young and Old Can Find Common Ground' concluded that people of all generations share the same values, but they define and express them differently.[28]

Those values are family, integrity, achievement, love, competence, happiness, self-respect, wisdom, balance, and responsibility.

---

[28] 'Retiring the Generation Gap: How Employees Young and Old Can Find Common Ground', Deal, Jennifer J., (J-B CCL (Center for Creative Leadership)), John Wiley & Sons, 2007

"The generations don't differ in what they value; they differ in how they demonstrate those values," says Deal.

One of the things people want, no matter their age, is to be respected. What they mean by respect varies, however. To some, it means, 'Listen to me and pay attention to what I'm saying.' To others, it means, 'Give my opinions the weight I feel they deserve' or 'Do what I tell you to do.'

"Older people primarily talked about respect in terms of 'give my opinions the weight I believe they deserve' and 'do what I tell you to do'," reports Deal.

"Younger respondents characterized respect more as 'listen to me and pay attention to what I have to say'."

People of all ages have an idea in their mind of how others should treat them. When the behavior of others doesn't conform to that expectation, they feel disrespected.

"It is his or her failure to meet expectations that is upsetting."

Older people often found it challenging to work with younger people, who seemed to be less respectful towards management than their older colleagues thought appropriate. Younger people felt older workers didn't take them seriously because they lacked experience.

This is where communication is so vital. For instance, if those older and younger colleagues were able to ask each other, "What's your biggest challenge around the issue of respect?" they might discover what behavior each considered to be 'respectful' and 'disrespectful'. Once they understood, the likelihood is they'd adapt their behavior.

Chapter 6

RHB In Action Breaking Down Barriers

Corporate turnaround specialist, Steve Malinowski used RHB to help knock down silos, boost employee engagement and retention, and thereby raise productivity and profits in two major organizations: Janes Family Foods, quality provider and innovator of frozen products, and the Kraus Group, one of North America's largest integrated carpet and flooring manufacturers.

As a corporate turnaround specialist, Steve inevitably ends up at companies in which there is some logistical, operational or manufacturing-type challenge.

"I spend most of my time sorting that out and getting the company back on track," he says. Such was the case at Janes.

In many ways, Janes had been a great Canadian success story, with some operational and financial success, but when Steve arrived, a major new product line had been introduced, and it was not going well. On top of that, they had just expanded and built a brand new flagship manufacturing plant, and that also was not performing well.

The situation had created friction among departments and taken its toll on staff morale and retention.

"When I first got to Janes, we had a salaried workforce turnover of about 50%. People found it a tough place to work."

The stress of the situation on the remaining employees had fueled a blame culture.

"The stress on the organization at the time was pushing people into a 'cover my tail' kind of mentality. It seemed that most people were interested in fault rather than contribution. They were looking for who to blame.

"The more there was a blame culture, the more people would retreat into departmental silos and point the finger at other departments.

"There were silos between production and quality. There were silos between what I would call product engineering and marketing too.

"Traditionally, the conflict between design engineering and marketing is legendary. At Janes, our marketing team wanted a product that was the greatest thing since sliced bread. Of course, the product design engineers would say 'Well, unfortunately, the product you've described would defy the laws of chemistry and physics. Therefore, we cannot make a product that lives up to that.'

"There was any number of heated discussions where marketing people would say things like 'Maybe we just need better product design people.' That would, in turn, make people defensive.

The product design people would respond with comments like 'Maybe we need more realistic marketers.'

"That sort of dialogue would go back and forth. That was the kind of environment I had walked into and even though the company had significant market success, there were any number of silos between the different functional groups.

"We needed to find a way of eliminating that friction, breaking down those silos so that we could head back towards executing what was already a reasonably good strategy.

"The thing with silos in any organization is that unless people are confronted with behavior and faced with the consequences of that behavior on mutual goals, it continues."

The company had a profit-sharing plan for all its employees, but the functional silos were so entrenched that they superseded that.

"At Janes, everyone was legitimately and sincerely interested in seeing the company succeed in terms of market share and profitability, but the notion of trying to defend one's silo somehow superseded the mutual goals that people sincerely believed in. That's how powerful silos can be.

"The culture was more focused on blame than contribution, more focused on 'How I look' rather than what we achieved. It was a culture that was more interested in receiving rather than doing something because it was a good thing to do."

It was obvious something drastic needed to be done to bring about wholesale behavioral change.

"One of my HR people had been at a conference at which you spoke, and she said, 'Steve, this is the guy that we need to come here. With all the good cultural things that we're doing, it would be great to have Dave come in and speak and give this whole thing some spark and some life.'"

So not long afterward, I went in to talk to employees at Janes.

"The point was to kickstart the whole self-evaluation of how one, in fact, behaves. What Dave allowed us to do was to get people to stop for a morning and just do some self-examination.

"RHB introduced really simple, memorable language that allowed people to reference that type of behavior in a way that didn't make others defensive. The way Dave presented it made it less about labeling someone, and more about labeling a behavior.

"It almost forces people to stop for a second and elevate the conversation back to the higher level things everyone can agree on, and then drop down to finding out where they don't actually agree.

"It's a lot like negotiations with unions. You sit at a table with union reps, and you have a disagreement over something. The way you get through that is to elevate the conversation back up to what you're all trying to achieve together as a company. Once you have agreement on those high-level aspirations, you can start talking about what can be done together to achieve those things.

"The RHB language around first, second and third gear is very sticky, in that it allows people to talk about that in a way that doesn't directly threaten identity.

"In Dave's training, he went to great lengths to explain that you're not labeling the person but the behavior. In so doing, the level of defensiveness ends up being reduced considerably. Some people are going to be defensive anyway, but they're the people that you're going to have to remove from your organization.

"The reason that RHB is sticky is that it actually teaches people and gives them a mechanism for understanding why it's non-threatening. 'I'm not calling you a bad guy. I'm calling what you just said a bad behavior. It's a bad behavior coming from an otherwise good guy. Can we talk about why you said that and what's driving it?' That's a totally different thing."

The RHB approach was universally accepted.

"There wasn't resistance to the idea. Dave's talk gave people enough of a personal shakeup they had to rethink how they were behaving.

"The genius of the RHB approach, I would say, is that it gives people the language and almost the authority to call someone on a behavior without threatening the identity of the person they're speaking to."

It helped to eliminate the friction that had existed between employees and departments.

"For example, when we dealt with behavioral problems between quality and production, we could easily sit down and talk to people and say 'Listen, this is first gear behavior, and this is second gear behavior. As we already know, that's not productive. You are a good person, and you add enormous value to this organization. However, some of the ways in which you are behaving are the behaviors that we don't want.'

"Gradually, they'd start to say things like, 'Guys come on, that's a first gear 'What's in it for me?' type statement. You're not thinking of the bigger picture.' That would lead into a more productive discussion about the bigger picture and what were we trying to achieve.

What's more, the effects proved long-lasting.

"At Janes, the whole concept of breaking down silos and third gear concept was very sticky. So sticky in fact that even when I left the company, three years later, employees were talking to other employees and saying things like, 'Hey, don't say stuff like that. That's first gear.'"

The RHB approach was also integrated into the company's performance management evaluation system so that it incorporated an attitude and behavior type of dimension as well as job competence.

"When I started at Janes, the performance evaluation system consisted of annual reviews. They were either entirely project oriented or job competence oriented and had nothing to do with attitude, values or behavior.

"They vacillated between, on the one hand, a highly subjective, really loose, almost meaningless exercise where everyone got a slight pat on the head, and nothing ever really of substance was talked about, to the other extreme which was the engineering approach, where every personal behavior had some type of measurement and metric associated with it. Each one of fifty different activities was weighted towards a person's eventual score. Their score determined where they got ranked on their final ranking system.

"The first one was so loose that it made no impact on anyone's behavior at any time. The second was too rigid and strict, and required one to apply numbers to things that were not inherently numeric.

"It meant if a Corporate VP was doing a fantastic job in terms of delivering business results but operating in their division in a way that was indistinguishable from a dictator, he or she might have a performance evaluation in which attitude was worth two percentage points, so even if they scored zero for attitude, they'd still score 98% for everything else. What behavior would change as a result of that evaluation? None.

"We simplified the system so that it was based on two dimensions: one of which was 'Business Results Achievement', and the other dimension was called 'Values-Attitude-Behaviour'. Yes, we actually evaluated people on how they operated on a regular basis in terms of their gear.

"The better they did in terms of being in third gear more frequently, the better they would score on that dimension."

Under the new system, a group of managers rather than one manager would be responsible for every employee's performance evaluation.

"It was still reasonably subjective. But we eliminated a lot of subjectivity by having people's evaluations done by a small group of managers rather than just a single manager.

"Take the Quality Assurance Department as an example. The QA manager would be one of the managers evaluating the QA people, but there'd also be the production manager as well as the maintenance manager and the sales manager.

"That's because the QA people had customer-supplier relationships with all those people. By having those four people, who would have interacted with the QA people on a regular basis, get together in a room and, mediated by HR, have a real discussion about each one of say a dozen QA people as to how they're actually behaving in terms of first, second and third gear allowed it to be significantly more objective than subjective."

The new system was introduced at the beginning of a fiscal year. Instead of just having an annual performance review, every employee would have monthly half-hour one-on-one meetings with their direct manager.

They'd also have a mid-year formal performance review. "During this meeting, employees would be told what they'd done that managers were thankful for. Their managers would also detail the things that they needed to work on for the last half of the year."

A year-end review would also take place.

"That had two dimensions to it: their Values-Attitude-Behaviour, based on how well they are doing in which gear, and their job performance: Did they do the things they said they would get done?"

Their performance in those two dimensions was then plotted on a graph.

"We recognized that we had some people who'd gotten the job done but who had a very poor attitude. We had to work with them on their behavior.

"We also had people who had great attitude and behavior but who didn't get the job done. That was also unacceptable. We had to work on their job competence.

"There was another group who didn't have a great attitude and didn't get the job done. Frankly, those people were exited.

"But much to our surprise and delight, we had a lot of individuals who had excellent behavior as well as excellent job competence.

"Year after year, as we did this, more and more people ended up in that top quadrant. Fewer and fewer people ended up in the bottom left quadrant, because they had come to understand that behavior mattered.

"Those who couldn't change, left: either we initiated it, or they initiated it. Either way, they left because they didn't fit."

That whole program went on for about three years.

"So from the first time that we engaged Dave to the time that I left the company—and I left the company only because we got acquired by a larger competitor— we doubled our sales and doubled our market share. Before that, the company had a good reputation in the market and with consumers, but had plateaued.

"We introduced some good products that were really well targeted so that the product design and the marketing of what they were supposed to do were extremely coherent. We had very few new product failures.

"I would say that's a direct result of Dave's presentation. Instead of people wasting their energy on battling for power for their silos, they were turning that energy towards a mutually acceptable goal.

"We weren't doing that before. RHB language gave us a productive way of calling each other out so that we could put that behind us in any given meeting and move forwards towards a mutually acceptable goal.

"If we had spent those four years continuing to battle each other within the company, we would have never been able to achieve the things that we did.

"It was a significant result of breaking down silos and understanding the impact of personal behavior and attitude in the way teams work together, especially cross-functional teams but even within teams.

"The more we take our limited amount of energy and stop wasting it on destructive stuff and start putting it on constructive stuff the better we're going to be. That's exactly what happened at Janes.

"Now, because of the success of the company—we had increased sales, profitability, and market share— we increased in attractiveness to a buyer. Our owner and founder, Mr. Janes, had gotten to the point where he was thinking of retiring, so it was a natural conclusion anyway.

"Certainly, creating a company in which the financial performance and the operational performance was heavily influenced by our cultural performance made for a very attractive proposition for several different acquirers.

"Had we not even been acquired, there are two ongoing competitive advantages that our cultural change brought us, one of which was that we became the kind of employer that people were desperate to come work for, and no one wanted to leave."

Staff turnover had undergone a dramatic slowdown.

"In the last two years I was there, I think we had one retirement, and one person left us. That was it. Several people in the organization were headhunted by our competitors, and although they were offered more money, they chose to stay.

"Our second strategic advantage was that we spent our energy achieving our goals rather than in internal fighting.

"That's a huge, huge competitive advantage. If you can break down silos, so people work together towards a mutually agreed upon goal, then you are ahead of 99% of other companies.

"You help a company transform its culture into one that spends its energy creating value as opposed to wasting its energy destroying value internally.

"From the time that Dave started working with us to the time that I left Janes, we doubled our sales, and almost doubled our profit.

"Now, that's great, but it's certainly not the kind of thing that I can attribute directly to breaking down silos and third gear behavior. The change in culture was, however, the enabler for some of that stuff to happen.

"The cultural transformation we underwent at Janes, and our ability to use third gear for teaching language and breaking down silos, enormously reduced the amount of friction that was there.

"Even when conflict did arise, which happens when you've got a bunch of highly motivated passionate people together in a room, it acted a little like oil in the system to help us reduce the friction so we could actually get past it and move onto the work in concert we needed to do.

"So for every dollar and for every hour of investment into the company, a larger percentage went towards us moving the business forward as opposed to overcoming the internal friction. That is an enormous, enormous competitive advantage.

"If you've got a healthy culture with less friction and silos working with rather than against each other, do you not think that will translate into better performance? Of course, it will."

After leaving Janes, Steve was appointed CEO and President of the Kraus Group in March 2013. Although it had been a successful family-owned business for many years, the global recession and housing crisis in the US had pushed the company deep into debt.

That prompted the departure of the founding Kraus family from the ownership ranks in 2012.[29] Hilco UK Ltd., a British private equity firm specializing in fixing distressed businesses, bought the company's debt from

[29] '*New boss hoping to take Kraus on magic carpet ride*', Lee, Peter, *Guelph Mercury*, Metroland Media Group Ltd., www.guelphmercury.com, Mar 16, 2013

three secured lenders, then began the process of turning it around from bankruptcy.

The company's unionized workers had also agreed to wage and benefit concessions to help Kraus get through the crisis.

"When I arrived at Kraus, it had spent five years in a death spiral and ended up in bankruptcy," he says.

He spent the first few weeks getting to know employees and customers.

"I'm not a knee-jerk kind of manager. I'd rather get immersed in the business, meet all the folks, meet all the customers and try to find out where we stand and then develop a strategy."

He went around and shook hands with every worker on all three shifts in the Waterloo plant and was impressed to learn that many have been at the company for 20 or 30 years.

It soon became evident that the five years of uncertainty about the company's future had had a devastating impact on morale.

"The people who had stayed had been through the wringer; they had been emotionally wrung out by the whole 'Do I have a job? Do I not have a job?' thing over five years."

It had created a culture of fear and blame.

"There was widespread fear in the company that we would not survive.

"Culturally, it was very dysfunctional because of the financial struggles. It was a relatively entrenched blame-game type culture. People had retreated into what I call their own little 'What's in it for me?' shells.

"It was understandable that people would try to deflect blame and cover their tracks and figure how to dodge the bullet, because if they wanted to continue with their job they obviously needed to figure out who else's fault it must have been.

"Once upon a time, Kraus had been very successful, but as the company's performance deteriorated over time, people's behavior became worse.

"They'd lost confidence in the company and in themselves," he says. "Defeat was all they had known for years. It had also become self-defeating, in the sense that anytime anything went wrong, people circled their own wagons and tried to figure out how to deflect blame, rather than actually solving the problem."

He wanted to give them hope and convince them the company could be turned around, so effort was put into communication, through town hall meetings and other meetings, to make sure people on the production lines and throughout the company understood what the company was trying to achieve in terms of the quality of the product and relationships with customers.[30]

"Here at Kraus we had an operational turnaround to complete, we needed to fix what we were actually doing, and we had to have a financial turnaround in short order."

---

[30] *'Turnaround at Kraus depended on engaging people behind the scenes, manufacturers told at summit'*, Simone, Rose, The Record, www.therecord.com, Jun 24, 2015

The company was reorganized, and divisions were consolidated to simplify the structure. Some processes were also changed so supervisors had their own leadership teams to represent the people on the lines.

At Kraus, this was accomplished by decentralizing supervision and creating leadership teams that involved workers at all levels.

"Fundamentally we needed to have a cultural turnaround. Culture is more than just a few feel-good moments," he says. "It is the sum of employees' discretionary efforts. We don't need *some* employees to *sometimes* go the extra mile. We need *all* employees to go the extra inch *every day*.

"We had to start that cultural change from scratch because a lot of basic behaviors that one would find in a modern company had never been cultivated."

For example, the company had never used a formal performance evaluation system. That's changed since Steve's arrival.

"We are doing performance evaluations for the first time in the company's 50-year history. It's a very new concept."

Knowing the positive impact RHB had on behavior at Janes, Steve asked me to talk with his new team.

"Dave's talk was a bit of a revelation to our folks. Interestingly enough, it had an enormous, enormous immediate impact. One person came up to me afterward and said, 'I have been to hundreds of these corporate speech things, and I've never had anything that has both shaken me and given me optimism like Dave did.'

"I thought that was good. It shook people out of the status quo. The number of comments and thank you cards that we both received afterward was staggering."

That was only the start, however. Steve then asked me to provide coaching and to work with the company's HR department to make sure the change in behavior lasted.

"Through some additional coaching and some amazing work from our HR department to develop and institutionalize a number of supporting programs, we've been able to get much more traction with people around things like attitude and behaviour and why they matter."

That has had an impact on the bottom line.

"We have increased sales by about 45% over three years. We have gone from being bankrupt to being solidly profitable."

By 2015, sales had grown by 17% in a year compared with the industry average of 3%. "So we took away a significant amount of market share (from competitors), and we improved our bottom line by $10 million in the space of two years.

"So the impact again is there. What RHB helped us to do was break down interdepartmental silos that were a problem, for example, between Sales and Production. Inevitably there was friction between them because Sales felt that Production didn't produce what Sales wanted, or the quality wasn't good enough or something along those lines.

"Sales would say 'We can't sell because you guys aren't making the right product.' Production would say 'Well, you're not telling us which product we should make so we're just guessing.'

"It was a circular blame game."

RHB also helped give individual employees more self-confidence.

"It helped us address that kind of behavior, but I think more than anything it helped us to address the mental silos that people had.

"They were self-labelling. When you've got a company that was beaten down so badly over five years and ended up in bankruptcy, the people who had gone through that were survivors, but they had a combination of survivor guilt and a feeling that somehow they deserved their fate.

"That mental silo of 'Yeah, we do suck' had to be broken down, and the RHB approach of using first, second and third gear helped people. They learned that, in the same way that you don't label people in other departments, you don't label yourself, your own department, your own company, because the labels are destructive."

Employees realized their mindset and behavior had an influence on the company's success or failure.

"People realized their behavior was inextricably linked to their identity and, the more they behaved as if the company was a market loser, the more it became a market loser. The more they behaved as if the company was a market winner, the more it actually became a market winner.

"We started to use a new language around what we were doing. It was a more positive language. People understood that our core identity was not one of a bankrupt company. Bankruptcy was just a phase we passed through. Our core identity for 50 years had been a company that was extremely successful, and we were now on the way back there.

"Here's a perfect example of that: In the five years before I arrived, when the company was deteriorating, it introduced five new products. That's five products in five years.

"When I came onboard, it was apparent the product line was stale and dated. It needed refreshing. People were like 'Okay, what product are we going to add this year?'

"I said, 'We're not going to add one product, we're actually going to do 40.' We launched 40 new products in that first year, 35 in the second year, and 26 in the third year.

"Now, when I told people we were going to launch 40 new products in that first year, they said there was no way it would happen. The wagons were circling, the silos had already formed in their mind that we were incapable of doing it.

"We were able to break down those silos, again referencing back to your talk. We said, 'Let's stop labeling ourselves and the different departments. Let's work together and see what success we have.'

"I'd come from the food business and to put this into perspective, when you introduce ten new products, you expect only three to be on shelves in the supermarket in a year's time. Three out of ten is a pretty good success rate.

"Well, we introduced 40 new products in that first year and of the 40 new products, we had 30 on shelves at the end of the year. It was amazing."

That success brought about a different kind of stress, however.

"Unfortunately, despite the fact we had talked about how we needed to be ready for success, no-one really believed it would happen. When we introduced 40 new products and 30 turned out to be really good, we had orders coming out of our ears.

"We scrambled and scrambled to try and figure how we were going to produce all those orders. Production had risen by 67% by the middle of that first year.

"That induced all kinds of stress on the organization—production couldn't keep up, and suppliers couldn't keep up.

"It also introduced a whole new level of friction within the company. We're only now coming to the end of the phase of dealing with that.

"But it's improving. I was at a customer event last night and was talking to one of our sales guys, and he said, 'I remember when you came and did your first meeting with all the sales guys, and you said one of your goals was to try to make Kraus a place where it's fun to work. We all walked away and thought, "What is that guy smoking? He's another one of those rah-rah cheerleader types."

"We didn't believe you. We thought that it was a whole lot of nonsense, but I haven't had this much fun at work in decades.'

"I asked him why, and he said, 'Look around, Steve, at our customers. They love us here. They love our products. Our sales have grown 45% just in this last year with this group. We're making money again. This is a lot of fun.'"

Chapter 7

RHB in Action Boosting Engagement

Nicolas Heldmann is the Vice-President of Accounting Services at OpenText Corporation, Canada's largest developer of enterprise information management software. He used RHB combined with Six Sigma to bring about a transformation within his company's accounting services department.

A few years ago, Nicolas, who's been with OpenText for nearly 20 years, was tasked with leading a finance transformation productivity initiative across a newly merged Accounting Services department.

"I had the opportunity to lead a fairly sizeable group of 140 people in a newly formed department," he recalls.

"We were changing people's jobs and potentially even eliminating certain roles and responsibilities, with the intention of creating more value-add positions and shifting the work.

"We knew it had to be done from the perspective of things like efficiency, scalability, and profitability.

"From a leadership perspective, we knew we had to do things differently than we had in the past. So we were looking for new approaches; a new dynamic that had an appeal for staff."

That's when Nicolas thought of inviting me to address his newly-formed team.

> "We were starting off on the path of this transformation and thinking how to keep people really engaged and really motivated. I first heard you talk about eight years ago. I remember I found the whole concept of the three gears very, very appealing.
>
> "We thought it would be a really good time to engage you to see how we could create a program focused on customer service using the RHB concepts.
>
> "We needed to get people focused on doing the right thing for the right thing's sake and to put all other worries aside. We wanted them to focus on our internal and external customers."

The program was a combination of RHB and Six Sigma and Lean.

> "We based the program loosely on the four main principles of Six Sigma: looking at a process end to end, ensuring that you've got metrics so that you can measure things, ensuring that it's customer-centric and ensuring that change is driven by the subject matter experts or front line staff.
>
> "It was really those last two principles that have stuck with us. Our frontline folks are not only buying into the changes, but they are driving the changes. They've got the ideas, and they know their jobs the best.

"We wanted to know how we could bring that out for the benefit of the customer. That was when we brought Dave in. We wanted him to launch a program that was specifically focused on customer service and doing the right thing for the customer.

"The idea was that if we focused on the customer (and that includes our internal customers too) and figured out their pain point, that would naturally lead to further process improvement. It's tied in with the whole notion of continuous improvement.

"The real appeal of the RHB concept was that it was so universal and so easy to understand. RHB has a place as a philosophy to bring people together and appeal to doing the right thing for the customer, doing the right thing for the process, and putting a lot of the silo turf wars behind you.

"It really fitted well with the new approach to leadership that we had adopted where we were putting our people first.

"I think the challenge we all face is that when you get up higher in the management ranks there's a belief that a solution needs to be complex rather than straightforward. We all tend to gravitate to very difficult principles. But RHB is really straightforward.

"Once you know how you can integrate the RHB philosophy with your company's vision, mission, and values, I firmly believe there's room for it.

"It is such an appealing concept, and it really fitted with our transformation and the principles of lean and Six Sigma."

I spoke with Nicolas's employees and found that they immediately understood the RHB three gears concept.

"It was an instant hit with our folks. It was absolutely wonderful to have something that was so aligned with what we were doing. It really felt like a well thought out process, and it dovetailed so well into the Lean and Six Sigma principles.

"As much as we were using the Lean and Six Sigma principles, the philosophy of RHB was the appeal. People really got the idea of doing the right thing for the customer.

"Our headcount pretty much stayed flat for the better part of four years, but revenue almost doubled in size in that time."

That is due to the winning combination of Lean and Six Sigma and the RHB approach.

"It was a great partnership, a great combination. Lean and Six Sigma are proven methodologies, but the RHB philosophy meant people were truly engaged. It certainly made a large contribution to our efficiency savings.

"Even years later, people are still quoting the RHB gears."

Now...Break Down the Barriers in your Company

If you'd like to break down the barriers or silos in your company and increase your employees' engagement, then book Dave Howlett to present a seminar, workshop or keynote address.

With a 30-year background in sales, business development, and leadership, Dave brings a wealth of business knowledge and human behavior to his humorous and thought-provoking keynote speeches and workshops. He is also a Distinguished Toastmaster and a multiple Ironman athlete.

Each RHB keynote address is customized to reflect the vision of senior management and to suit the audience. They're offered in lengths of 20 minutes to three hours and can include multimedia, audience participation, and a Q&A session. You can also choose a workshop in a two-hour, half-day and full day format.

Dave has spoken to hundreds of audiences in the corporate, government and association fields.

For information, call 1-416-209-1503

or email info@realhumanbeing.org.

The sooner you book, the sooner your organization can reap the benefits of having an engaged, collaborative workforce.

What People Say About RHB & Dave Howlett

"Dave Howlett's 'Knocking Down Silos' presentation delivers not only better ways to network and talk to people but more even more: how to live a better life. Any leader in any company needs to have these skills in order to help make their departments better—and therefore, help the company to be better—since a company is simply the people who work for it. I'd recommend Dave to anyone looking to break their team out of a routine, and get them looking outside of themselves and the company."

Stephen Smith – Former President and CEO,
WestJet and Air Canada's ZIP

"As a lawyer with one of Canada's top law firms, my relationships with clients and associates are crucial to my career. Dave's talks have shown me to: 1. Pay attention - listening is a good thing. 2. Be enthusiastic about others' successes. 3. Be reliable! (and admit it honestly when you are not). 4. Always help others."

Vanessa Grant – Partner, McCarthy Tetrault LLP

"We interviewed a number of potential trainers for our annual internal sales conference. Dave Howlett customized his RHB material to suit the needs of our audience and leveraged real-world applications of the RHB behavior modification process. In fact, our president said that she had never witnessed a presentation that actively engaged participants at this level during a multi-hour period. I would recommend Dave Howlett and RHB to any company that wants to attract new clients and strengthen their existing relationships."

William Buzzeo - Senior VP of Cegedim

"I recently attended 'Knocking Down Silos' with Dave Howlett, and I was truly inspired, and determined to make a difference not only in my career but also in my personal life and get into 3ʳᵈ gear.

"I am an account executive with a large Motivational and Improvement Agency that constantly looks for and books new and interesting guest speakers, and I can assure you the Dave Howlett is someone I would book for both internal meetings as well as corporate events.

"He engages his audience from the moment he steps to the microphone and incorporates humor and interacting with the audience throughout the presentation. The audience was encouraged to get out of their comfort zone, and to compliment, find a commonality, and challenge each other which everyone could relate to and could take away with them moving forward in everyday situations.

"I would highly recommend Dave for any upcoming meetings and conferences when you need a truly memorable speaker that will have everyone talking and making positive changes to gain success."

Dana Warren - Maritz Canada Inc.

"In his two-hour seminar, Dave managed to effectively deliver the same concepts that I had learned during nine months of personal coaching."

Cristian Mandachescu - VP, Trade Finance and Financial Institutions
ScotiaBank

"At the last presentation, I sat in the back, like I always do. Dave challenged us all to talk to some people around us. I did. Guess what? I made a contact that I have stayed in touch with ever since. It turns out that both of us are 'reluctant networkers'. We meet regularly for coffee and to encourage each other. Thank you, Mr. Connector!"

Jim Love - Managing Partner, Performance Advantage

"A quick follow-up note to tell you how much I enjoyed your presentation last night. You kept things moving, had lots of valuable information, and the humor was refreshing. I connected with a couple of students during the breakouts and had interesting connections with both."

David Lewis - The LoweMartin Group

"I've been to dozens, if not hundreds, of these kinds of seminars, where speakers wax on eloquently about how to network and how to build a solid Rolodex and how to find leads and sales prospects. I'm not a businessperson or a salesperson, so I usually just write about the event—if it's important to my readers—and then forget about any information I may have picked up there. It just doesn't help me much in my capacity as a journalist and editor—or as a person in general. Howlett actually had some great ideas about creating opportunities—ideas that just might change my life."

P.J. Harston - National Business Editor, Sun Media

"We are surrounded by well-meaning professionals who, no matter how they try, sometimes can't avoid making us feel behind or inadequate because they say we are training too hard, not training enough, training incorrectly or ... whatever. I very much appreciate your 'level playing field approach' to your audience in that you do not position yourself as having seen the light when [the audience members] remain in the dark, and you are the one holding the flashlight."

Evan Thompson - Partner, Thompson, Wiley + Associates

"I went to Dave's seminar 'Knocking Down Silos'. It started at 6:30 p.m. and ran until just after 9:00 p.m. I thought: 'Are you kidding me? – what's he going to talk about for 2 and a half hours!!!' Given my deficient attention span, I was particularly worried about lasting the duration.

"Turns out, the night flew by, and I have to say, I was completely 'wowed' by Dave, his interaction with the audience and the presentation itself. It was one of the best networking/sales seminars I have ever been to and every person I met or spoke with in attendance shared that sentiment. I met some really interesting people, who because of Dave, were looking for ways to help me, whether it be in business or with a personal challenge. The concepts presented are easy, genuine, self-rewarding and can be implemented immediately.

"At the end of the presentation, I thought I would wait around and say a quick hello to Dave. By just after 10:00, he was still surrounded by people from the audience, who wanted to meet or speak with him, so I never had the chance. It was unbelievable - talk about 'magnetic'!

"For anyone who has the opportunity to hear Dave speak in the future, invest the time because it is definitely worth it."

Allison Bryce - Partner, The MAGNES Group Inc.

"I am part of a group of senior executives who had Dave in to talk with us. This is not an easy group to impress. We were very glad to have had Dave speak to us, and we are better off for it.

"For me, when someone can inspire fresh thinking on a topic you thought had been beat to death, he deserves a lot of credit.

"Often, when the topic is networking, you are told by the speaker how important it is, but somehow, when the speaker is done, you really don't feel any more prepared than before to be good at it. This may create a little hesitation when asked to attend another seminar on networking. All I can say is: put your concerns aside.

"Dave Howlett does not waste your time telling you what you already know - networking is a key to success. What Dave does is help you become a better networker by giving you very pragmatic advice and by giving you an opportunity to practice what you've learned in a low-risk, constructive environment.

"It is no surprise that Dave has coined the term RHB - Real Human Being - since that is how Dave lives and that is what would resonate with him.

"Whether you are new to networking, an old hand at it, or not even yet convinced it is right for you, you owe it to yourself to attend Dave's seminar on Knocking Down Silos. You'll be glad you did. Thanks, Dave.

Richard Cantin

"Dave, you are awesome. Thank you for sending the lecture summary over, it will always stay on my wall as a reference. Our Master of Biotechnology Program is so much better because of your participation in our seminars. I will definitely forward to my friends and colleagues so they won't miss out. I will schedule my calendar for your next talk!"

John Tang - PDS Quotations & Business Planning, Patheon Inc.

"In my 27-year career in the investment industry, I have heard and participated in many workshops, seminars, and presentations. Dave Howlett's amazing 2 1/2 networking 'Knocking Down Silos' event was fantastic!

"Seldom does a speaker capture my attention for long periods of time. Dave was the exception. Dave Howlett's presentation was captivating, interesting and fun. The best parts? I learned something, made some contacts and walked away invigorated!"

Deborah Eaton-Kent CFA – Training and Development Consultant

"We can learn all we want from books, but real life is a school in its own right. Dave teaches street smarts; he walks the talk. His seminars are invaluable to anyone who wants to make a success of his/her professional and personal lives. The results will speak for themselves."

Coenraad Claassens Servier

"I currently work for a large pharmaceutical company in a sales capacity, and over my four years with the company, we have been bombarded with 'motivational seminars' meant to inspire us and to motivate us to become, well, better employees for the company. Your talk was different in that it promoted self- improvement for the sake of bettering and appreciating one's own life and ambitions, and for that I thank you."

MF

"I brought my younger sister (24 yrs) and my dad (55 yrs) and you managed to inspire them both equally! Your talk truly crosses all generations."

Diane Stogiannes Dofasco

"Your networking talk was full of useful information, lively, and upbeat; the inclusion of your professional and personal accomplishments in your introduction immediately set you into the context of someone who has a message and who has, and who continues to earn respect. Your follow-up of an emailed PDF to all participants is remarkable."

Dr. Ulrich J. Krull - Professor of Analytical Chemistry, and AstraZeneca Chair in Biotechnology, Vice-Principal: Research, University of Toronto at Mississauga

"I'm in London right now working for Morgan Stanley, but I've already contacted several people in the Waterloo/Toronto area and am forcing them to go to your sessions. I've been raving about you and your sessions for a while, and now they've got a chance to hear you speak."

Dan Marantz - Morgan Stanley

"Thank-you for putting on a great seminar last night; your enthusiasm is very contagious! I met up with a couple of friends afterwards and couldn't stop talking about all the things that I'd learned. Although I'd already been to this seminar in the past, I thought it would be good to get a refresher."

Nicole Tingley - Torcan Chemical Ltd.

"Dave's talk will open your eyes to several critical skills you can use to impress your key contacts. He will teach you how to become a natural at adding value in your networking circles – so your colleagues will see you (and promote you) as an indispensable resource."

Dr. Nora Cutcliffe - BioPharma Consultant

"I left your "Knocking Down Silos" seminar completely energized about networking - the first time that has ever happened. I attribute this to the clarity and practicality of your presentation and the techniques you outlined. These are things I can easily incorporate into my business to be immediately more effective at marketing my services. I feel like my eyes have finally opened, and I can see things in a whole new way. Your talk gave me information unlike anything I learned in business school!"

Robert Steinbach, MBA, CFA - Workflow & Productivity Coach

"Dave Howlett is one of the most inspiring speaker/teachers I've heard. At the heart of Dave's message is the challenge for us to become a 'good guy'; thus, unwittingly transforming into a 'Renaissance Man'. You know, one of those divinely inspired beings who are on a mission to teach us about the wisdom of giving others 125% without 'assuming' returns. The metaphor Dave uses is driving on First, Second or—the very best—driving in full Third Gear, i.e., offering outstanding professional performance, maintaining health in the body/mind relationship and, key to his talk, the cultivation of a truly generous spirit.

Linda Hazelden

"Knocking Down Silos appealed to the scientific, IT and admin staff of Axiom Real-Time Metrics. It covered topics relevant to both personal and professional growth and did it in such a way that was informative yet entertaining, and engaging. It is immediately apparent that you practice what you preach Dave and have been very successful with it. Thank you for sharing your insight and passion!"

Sue Elliot - Director, Strategic/Scientific Consulting, Axiom Real-Time Metrics

"Mr. Howlett was the best professional speaker we have had here for over two years. I was impressed by the way he delivered the message that it became very appealing to not only the local students but those with an international background."

Julia Zhu - Brock University

"Thank you so much for coming to our Focus on Bio-Chem Careers event yesterday. Your session was fantastic! The students were engaged and motivated. Your presentation style makes it easy for the students to relate to the topic and truly understand the benefits of networking. I am already hearing the students saying great things about your session. You definitely made an impact. I welcome you to come on campus anytime."

Tracy Rogers – Seneca College

"For me RHB brings out a widened scope of possibilities and allowances vs. narrow mindedness. I learn so much from the vast array of posts from all over the world. I am learning that there are tolerable, and there are intolerable thought processes and how to tell the difference."

Pat Sumak-Knecht

"What sticks in my mind is when you told us about the thank you cards every week. Reminds me to appreciate everyone that enters my life, whether for a short or extended period. Everyone should be acknowledged for the good they do."

Melissa Gallant

"I recently heard Dave speak at Queens University. I was one of the Royal Military College Cadets that attended, and was not only impressed by the way he presents himself to an audience as a public speaker; I was amazed at his confidence and the way he actually reached out and impacted us as a group. It was an unbelievable, life changing experience and coming from an engineering student, I can confidently say that I have never learned more in a three hour lecture period!"

Eric Robb

"Dave, I was struck by how honest and refreshing your presentation was. You spoke about things that other people don't often talk about like doing the right thing simply because it is the right thing to do. One thing that I learned from your talk was how to connect with people on a deeper level, to go beyond conversations about the weather and learn about what really matters to people.

"This skill is invaluable both in business and personal relations. The ability to have empathy for other people and understand where they are coming from, embodied in the RHB perspective of assuming that everyone is intelligent, is a key component of emotional intelligence. A vast body of research backs up the conclusion that emotional intelligence accounts for about two-thirds of the competencies that distinguish top performers across all categories of jobs. Your presentation is the only one I have seen that in a very tangible way provides direction on improving one's emotional intelligence. It is without exaggeration that I say your presentation was life changing

Anna Hawkins

"What was different to me is that you do what you do because you live what you speak—it is not just words spewed they are words that I live by, and it was nice to know I am not alone."

Nadeen Bennett

"I saw Dave about five years ago. In advance of attending Dave's RHB discussion, I went into the presentation very skeptical. Another motivational speaker - yadda, yadda. I came away, very mindful of his concepts—and today, I still carry his words with me. Whether it is discussions with Senior Executives or with working teams, as long as I use the RHB approach, I am able to drive our initiatives forward. By applying this concept consistently over the years, it allowed me to build the credibility to, most recently, obtain executive support in implementing a very complex global initiative. This is something that I believe, if I hadn't applied the RHB concept over a number of years, I would not have otherwise been successful. Thank you, Dave, Thank you for RHB."

Sophia Pugh

"Dave I was taken with your presentation. With your honesty and with the reminder that we should all be kinder and better to each other without the expectation to gain."

Cindy Chessell Bonham

"Saw you first in '08 at WLU, then in Mississauga a couple of years later. I still remember thinking how easy and sensible your suggestions were. Look professional—take care of yourself. Everyone you know is your network. Don't make others look bad by being bad. Watch, your weekend, challenge. Thank-you cards—hand-written ones. And, of course, the three gears, which are emphasized on your FB wall daily. It changed my way of thinking completely."

Kellie Superina

"Dave's presentation engages the audience from start to finish. His honest approach and easy manner that isn't preachy and isn't marketing razzle dazzle.

"After outlining the philosophy of RHB, Dave brings it back around to how that impacts what your audience does daily. While Dave is doing the talking is it still a very thought provoking discussion as the audience is examining their recent responses to various situations & leaves the room with a different perspective on their response behaviors.

"For the majority of attendees, at the presentation, I went to found themselves pausing to consider where another person is coming from in their next encounter with someone and tempered their response according to the RHB mind-set.

"There was a lot of discussion in subsequent days of 'wow' moments when they felt a change in their own actions and reactions. The difference is palpable and rewarding.

"RHB thinking allows for more rewarding and productive employee communication with each other and department stakeholders that is very positive. It becomes easier and easier to become an RHB because it fosters respect and makes you look at your own motives for an action, question or response. I was also lucky enough to participate in an RHB workshop that spanned several weeks at my office that is continuing to reap rewards daily."

Elizabeth Newman

"It stood out because I wasn't expecting the message, 'You want to network? Be a decent human being.' It was all so incredibly un-fake. Also, after working at UW for three years, I now know why you called it 'knocking down silos'. Silos, silos everywhere."

Michael L Davenport

"WOW! I can honestly say that I have never been so pumped and enthusiastic after a networking seminar (or any other seminar for that matter) as I was last night. Even though I only started 'Virtually Working for You' 6 months ago, I have already learned the power of networking. However, until last night, I had not learned any 'valuable' networking tools. I'm already doing some of the things you mentioned, but the most valuable thing I learned is how to get myself remembered. Everyone likes to be valued for what they do and if I make others feel good about what they did for me then 'what goes around, comes around.' It makes perfect sense!"

Mary Judge, Virtually Working for You

"Looking at your videos, Dave, I find that you have the ability to talk TO the people and not AT the people. Although you follow guidelines during your chats, you have that element of spontaneity that fits in very well (corny jokes included...Don't omit them!)"

Pat Wylie

"RHB is universal, thought-provoking and really gets us to look at our behavior, how it impacts others and the way we interact in society."

Jacqueline Watty

"I remember feeling invigorated by your presentation, as it solidified our corporate culture into a definable, precise concept. It made me proud to work for my company, and mindful of your concepts even more so, going forward. I agree with Allison—I think of your message 'every single day'."

Deborah Burrowes

"I loved the simplicity of the gears as well as the one good assumption. Very good for remembering to be open and compassionate. 1,2,3 is a lot easier to remember than other more complicated codes of behavior."

Katherine Lazaruk

"'Un-fake' is a good description. Authentic, simple doable: the antithesis of most speakers in the genre. Content over hype. The three gears/levels of behavior vs. reward is an easy to remember, relate and repeat analogy. The thank you cards: I tried it, and it was very well received."

Steven Penner

"I really loved how easy it was to put into practice. A lot of times you go see speakers who make you want to go out and be a great person but do not provide the tools to do so. The RHB talk by Dave gave specific and easy things to do in order to make a difference without expecting anything in return. Both looking at your gears and watch your weekend challenge have been tools that have stuck with me since your talk over five years ago now."

Elissa Christine

"I think what's stuck with me the most from your talk is that being in 3rd gear means that you can do something for someone else (ex: letting them into your lane) because you feel that is the right thing to do, and the person's response (e.g. a thank you wave or lack thereof) is okay because you did what you felt was right. Six years+ after I saw you speak I still think about doing the right thing, and I really feel that it's profoundly impacted my life (professionally and personally) in a very positive way."

Kat Andr

"I first heard you at the University of Toronto leadership conference. Instantly I connected to the message and it help me understand what I had been aiming for naturally my whole life. I used what I learned from Dave during interviews, networking, and day-to-day life. I am grateful to have experienced this message and have since introduced most of my family and friends to Dave. In fact, I'm heading up the organization committee for an upcoming fundraiser and couldn't have had anyone else speak but Dave. He was generous enough to donate his time to our event which is expected to sell out (500 people). Thanks Dave for spreading goodness throughout the world; you're a good guy."

Samar Qureshi

"I had the intention in my heart to be helpful to people, see the best in them and do my best to make them feel better for having run into me. Your presentation really drove those words from my heart and head into my daily actions. I became more aware of times when I wasn't 'living' those words. The three principles an RHB lives by, along with the concept of seeing situations in the context of the "three gears of behavior" raised my awareness, which in turn, provided me with a conscious choice to live in 3rd gear. Because that's who I really am! Still sending you thanks, many years after hearing your message!"

Michelle Romanica

"Dave—your presentation has awesome energy! You combine humor with many examples from real life situations. Your concept of the gears really resonates. You reach to the audience from the first moment and never let us snooze."

Karen Phillips

"I first heard you speak during a quarterly planning session with the rest of the planning group at the Engineering firm I work for. Your message of the gears resonated with me immediately. I was very new to the company and emotionally wounded from a terribly abusive relationship with my previous employer. As a mother the gears resonated at the perfect frequency, as an employee they restored my faith in humanity. The gears are simple and are what our parents taught us before the day and age of excessive technology and 24/7 work weeks. The concept of good guys and amazing women is exactly the type of world I want my children to grow up in. To say you have had an everlasting impact on my life both personal and professional is an understatement."

Leanne Tillaart

"The simple concepts especially 'assume everyone is intelligent' has made me more open to actively listening to others. This is really important in a workplace to have everyone take this approach. It will increase communication and creativity if people feel their ideas will be listened to with open minds."

Mike Bermingham

"The RHB experience is Paradigm shifting. From a business, cultural, religious perspective it helps build bridges of understanding and mutual cooperation, unlike any philosophy I have encountered. It's simple to understand and articulate three gears have given me a unique leverage on my competition, and market. It's incorporated into my elevator speech, my marketing presentations, and now it has become an essential part of my behavior. On top of that via social media, RHB is an interactive, engaged, diverse group of people who come together to assist each other in meaningful ways. There is nothing like it, and Dave Howlett in the world today. Fantastic organization, and personality."

Zeshan Mirza

"I first met Dave in my third year of college and when I was about to enter the 'real world'. I was in search of something and in search of how I as an individual was going to stand out in the interior design world. Dave invited me to one of his talks and not only did I learn a different way to lead my life with his RHB philosophy it also helped me in my personal life. Now that I have switched into a different career path I know his philosophy is transferable from different fields and different areas of my life.

"Overall I think RHB principles are an extremely valuable life lesson and way to live your life. He's also a cool guy!"

Melanie Alexander

"Recently I had the pleasure of meeting with Dave Howlett at an organized Corporate Event. Dave was one of our Guest Speakers, and his delivery of his topic was through humor and life experience. It was not a seminar or a lecture but a remarkable conversation.

"His message was simple, common sense self-awareness that made you want to take charge; join the conversation, listen and engage but most importantly recognize that we as RHBs are in charge of shifting gears.

"Dave inspired me to bring his message back to my workforce and share his 'good guy' philosophy with my General Manager along with the future implementation of a 'conversation with Dave' for our team and Retailers in the coming months.

"If you have an opportunity to meet Dave and listen to his message it will make sense and next time someone is giving you the gears you will be able to distinguish if they are in 1st, 2nd or 3rd gear and be able to respond accordingly.

"Who am I? I am a Marketing Manager of a retail shopping centre. Proudly, I am also an RHB whose self-awareness keeps me accountable of my own gear patterns."

MH

"In a two-hour 'lecture' Dave Howlett kept his audience captivated and on the edge of their seats. His talk was engaging, significant and interactive. Few professional educators or performers can sustain this level of audience engagement for this length of time. His ability to integrate meaningful, interactive exercises transformed his talk into an experience that re-shaped patterns of thought and behavior. That is the goal of education, of business, and of the arts. His unique ability to connect with his audience and connect them with one another is something I have rarely seen in my years in theatre- and education-related careers. What a gift!"

Aynne Johnston - Professor, Dramatic Arts, Queen's Faculty of Education

"I have been to other Networking Seminars where the presenter teaches you how to network within the confines of the room you are in. As soon as the conference ends so do all of the connections that you have made. With Dave Howlett's seminar, this will not happen.

"Using his unique approach and RHB concept Dave will lead you into learning networking by moving you into "the next gear." You will leave Dave's seminar not only able to network, but wanting to network. By using the RHB approach, other people will want to network with you. The RHB approach also means that once the network is established the participants want to continue it.

"This was demonstrated to me at a recent conference when a woman I had never met who had never heard of Dave came up and introduced herself to me. She told me that she had never done anything like this before, but after seeing Dave, she wanted to do it."

Ian J. Ferguson

"It gave me a new perspective on judging and categorizing people."

Suzanne Gabriel

"Dave - I have had the privilege of hearing more than one of your talks and not only do I find them motivational but more importantly down to earth. You provide the audience with practical concepts that relate in our everyday lives. You are a truly what you promote—a real human being."

Christine Walterhouse

"It's been six years since I first heard you speak Dave—it was at a leadership conference at UofT Mississauga. And I think what you said 'stuck' because it was honest, yet encouraged kindness and understanding. I believe what I was captured by personally was that no one else had explained it to us (as students) at that time the importance of having a 'real human' connection with people! You also taught us how a simple question—"what is your biggest challenge" —can be so captivating. And so reflective. Thanks for that, again!"

Aastha Sahni, RHB

"There is one thing I have got out of your talk many, many years ago, and its something I have lived by every since. 'You care less what others think when you realize how little they are thinking about you.' From that, I really stopped taking things personally and living in a self-centered world and realized everyone has their own battles in life. It changed my outlook on many things in life."

Nadia Saleem

"Thanks for your wonderful networking lecture yesterday in U of T. I am also impressed by your lifestyle, i.e. marathoner, businessman, teacher, and toastmaster."

Shumin Jin – MBA, Schulich School of Business

"Dave Howlett's 'Knocking Down Silos' workshop is one of the most memorable and practical workshops that I have ever been to. As a Consultant with Investors Group and essentially self-employed, the art of the introduction is extremely important to the viability and building of my practice. Having a solid and sound reputation is extremely important to me.

"Dave's workshop not only provided a very unique perspective on how to better introduce myself and to meet potential client's but also how to implement these techniques by way of speaking with others in attendance and learning how to use these techniques in a real life application right there at the workshop.   I am still using these techniques today and have encouraged many colleagues to attend this workshop should they have the chance.

Rob Wojtasik - Consultant, Investors Group Financial Services Inc.

"I have grown up reading books by Stephen Covey, Daniel Goldman, Anthony Robbins and have always taken something away from my reading, even if only for a short while. RHB is different. It sticks. For a long time. Even through major life changes. First, second and third gear resonated with me most, and they apply to every aspect of my life: professional, personal, family, friends, hobbies, driving, etc.

"Knowing the gears and working to apply the RHB principles in my life has improved my quality of life and the quality of relationships with those around me. They are a positive drop in the lake with the associated ripple effect. Four years on, the philosophies are still with me. They have been shaped through life experience and reinforced by positive results and a happier, more satisfying life. Dave is a 'nutritious' person to be around. That comes from a grounded, benevolent spirit. My wish is for the world to have more RHB's...more people practicing the principles and making positive contributions towards one another simply because it feels better to do."

Juli-Ann Sannuto, RHB

90318805R00078

Made in the USA
Columbia, SC
01 March 2018